Your Life is Re-markable

YOUR LIFE IS RE-MARKABLE

Becoming the you that's free to love

Jacqueline Scott

ELM HILL

A Division of
HarperCollins Christian Publishing

www.elmhillbooks.com

Your Life is Re-markable
Becoming the you that's free to love

Published in Nashville, Tennessee, by Elm Hill, an imprint of Thomas Nelson. Elm Hill and Thomas Nelson are registered trademarks of HarperCollins Christian Publishing, Inc.

Elm Hill titles may be purchased in bulk for educational, business, fund-raising, or sales promotional use. For information, please e-mail SpecialMarkets@ ThomasNelson.com.

Scripture quotations marked AKJV is taken from the American King James Version. Public domain.

Scripture quotations marked CEV are from the Contemporary English Version. Copyright © 1991, 1992, 1995 by American Bible Society. Used by permission.

Scripture quotations marked CSB˚, are taken from the Christian Standard Bible˚, Copyright © 2017 by Holman Bible Publishers. Used by permission. Christian Standard Bible˚, and CSB˚ are federally registered trademarks of Holman Bible Publishers.

Scripture quotations marked ESV are from the ESV˚ Bible (The Holy Bible, English Standard Version˚). Copyright © 2001 by Crossway, a publishing ministry of Good News Publishers. Used by permission. All rights reserved.

Scripture quotations marked KJV are from the King James Version. Public domain.

Scripture quotations marked NASB are from New American Standard Bible˚. Copyright © 1960, 1962, 1963, 1968, 1971, 1972, 1973, 1975, 1977, 1995 by The Lockman Foundation. Used by permission. (www.Lockman.org)

Scripture quotations marked NIV are from the Holy Bible, New International Version˚, NIV˚. Copyright © 1973, 1978, 1984, 2011 by Biblica, Inc.˚ Used by permission of Zondervan. All rights reserved worldwide. www.Zondervan.com. The "NIV" and "New International Version" are trademarks registered in the United States Patent and Trademark Office by Biblica, Inc.˚

Scripture quotations marked NLT are from the Holy Bible, New Living Translation. © 1996, 2004, 2007, 2013, 2015 by Tyndale House Foundation. Used by permission of Tyndale House Publishers, Inc., Carol Stream, Illinois 60188. All rights reserved.

Scripture quotations marked WEB are from the World English Bible˚. Public domain.

Library of Congress Cataloging-in-Publication Data

Library of Congress Control Number: 2019918919

ISBN 978-1-400328369 (Paperback)
ISBN 978-1-400328376 (eBook)

CONTENTS

DEDICATION

I would not be what I am...without you
With out your consistent care and grace
Without your love and desire to understand
Without your lifting of my eyes
Without your determination to overcome
Without His reminders through you of His overpowering love & purpose.
He has shaped me through you, molded me and blessed me utterly.
I love you. And I am getting to grow into our upper years together, watching things grey and fall and wrinkle
outwardly ... yet blossom, clarify and become young inwardly! Privileged to be yours...

Photo - Cassie Eubanks

Dan, you know, none of this would have been so without you.
You have waded with me through the mire of self, finding Him
even there! You and me always, Jackie

INTRODUCTION

Slumped on the side of my bed on the other side of the world, half-dazed, I wondered what I'd gotten myself into. I didn't know the language, had to pasteurize the milk and pick the little stones out of the rice. There were no disposable diapers and our fourth child needed one.

You know the you that you dream about being? The one who is a new and better version of who you are now, the version that your Maker intended? Why doesn't that just automatically happen? How do we become the person we were made to be? How do we get so off course?

Busy-ness, distraction and lack of direction try to keep us from growth. If we don't slow down and get some focus, we'll stay as we are or get worse. And we'll miss out on who we were supposed to be. Our souls need nurturing to grow, just like a garden, a child or an orchestra.

Foraging into this kind of growth takes time, thought and perseverance. Many abandon the effort leaving pieces of themselves scattered. Others attempt to assemble themselves and make good progress, then leave it because of the dark uneasy parts where everything fogs together with little clarity. Some actually get to a point of seeing a coherent, meaningful picture of why they are stuck or what their life is for.

My own growth seemed painfully slow and laborious. The disorientation and grind of cross-cultural living pushed me to deeper searching. I join many others on this quest of soul growth and hope to add another angle to the conversation.

CHAPTER 1

FINDING FEAR

"Fear God... and you will then have nothing else to fear."
From the hymn - Through All the Changing Scenes of Life

O ur little family had just moved to a foreign country that was in the throes of traumatic political upheaval. People were in shock trying to figure out how to live. Before the breakup of the Soviet Union, the government had provided everything; designated their job, their place and even what they were supposed to think. On the front of our son's first grade reading book from his Russian school were the words:  Lenin lived, Lenin lives, and Lenin will live. It was that deep. So, we were looking for ways to help these resilient yet floundering people.

My husband, Dan, was venturing to start a business to help show how entrepreneurship could be practiced honorably in a place where it was, until very recently, considered immoral. We hired services to help us register the business, later to find out they were corrupt. Our first clue was when they came to deliver the registration papers at the cold, leftover Soviet apartment that we used for an office, Oleg brought Tajir along with him. He was a Genghis Khan-looking fellow, the power-lifter type with close-cropped hair. Oleg sat down and went through the registration papers then gargled, "I want you to meet Tajir. He'll be your guard." Immediately Dan suspected what was going on and said, "I don't think we'll need him."

"Well," he threatened "bad things can happen..."

Taken aback and scrambling to fathom this new culture, Dan asked, "If we were to hire him what would we pay?"

"We'll come to an agreement...a percentage."

"A percentage of what?! We're just trying to get off the ground. We're in the red!" Not given easily to intimidation, Dan continued, "If we need a guard, I'll let you know; and he'll work for us."

Some days later, the office door opened abruptly and there was Tajir. He began to show up unannounced, making a habit of presumptuously walking into the office without knocking. Dan would greet him, tell him business was slow, practice his Russian, offer him tea, ask if he wanted to review the finances (still in the red), or study the Bible.... Tajir had a hard time keeping his smile under wraps. He was really a big teddy bear caught in this mafia mix. After a few weeks Oleg showed up and asked Dan why he wasn't paying Tajir. Dan curtly said, "If we want him, we will hire him."

Then the threats began. "Well, you have a wife and children..." Of course, this took it to another level. Dan showed them to the door, scarcely able to control his anger. In the post-Soviet power vacuum these types found ways of dealing with foreigners that clashed with ideals of ethical business.

Fear. It came closer to me that day! I recognized it, felt its power wanting to take me. I knew I had to make a choice. We had been warned that living here would be difficult and dangerous. As I wrestled, I had to lean on the rock-bottom belief that God is over all. I threw this like a hot potato to the God who wanted to show himself in this forsaken land. I had been working on taking my fears to him rather than denying or just bottling them as I had done over the years. For days its talons hulked over my mind and heart. I didn't want to live in fear and knew how it could keep me in a rut. I hated ruts but often found myself in them.

Fear had introduced itself to me decades before this. I recalled my first fear: death. "You mean everyone dies?" I remember thinking. This greatly troubled my little heart. I was about five years old and this was the first time that death had entered the chambers of my understanding. I couldn't quite get my mind around this one and I let it linger as I lay in one of the four bunks in the little bedroom of our row house in Missouri. We hadn't talked much about these kinds of things. There were four of us little ones with a dad in medical school and a mom trying to keep life together. So, I guess it got relegated to the back of my mind and life went on. Stealthily, fear came to my fragile heart that day and I was already becoming apt at the practice of pushing things to the back of my mind. That can be handy. But it comes back to bite. So here it was, trying to bite...

Our local business partner began to worry greatly about not accommodating Oleg and the day she brought it up, Dan happened to be wearing a T-shirt that said 'Fear Not'! Isaiah 41:10, ESV "Fear not for I am with you". Since it was winter and the city heat hadn't been turned on yet, he had his winter coat on over the T-shirt as he huddled over his desk. As he saw fear grasp Sasha's face, Dan remembered what he was wearing and yanked off his coat to show her the verse written on his shirt, a take-off of the then popular 'No Fear' logo. She got an ear-full about this God who was over all; much greater than this wanna-be mafia thug, and though she strained to listen, she still felt we needed to appease them. Being new in the culture, Dan decided to let her call the shots on this one. She called Oleg's office and planned to meet them to see what needed to be done.

The day came for the meeting and two local tour guides, inquiring about our new company, happened to come in for a consultation. Time got away as they discussed business. The phone rang. Sasha answering, looked worried and mouthed to Dan, "We're supposed to be at Oleg's office!" Dan asked her to reschedule, because we had unexpected clients arrive. This is an accepted cultural excuse due to their high value on hospitality, that whenever "guests came" it could trump another appointment. After this, Tajir inexplicably stopped showing up and we didn't hear from Oleg for weeks. One day Dan's other partner bumped into Oleg's secretary working at a different office. When he asked about Oleg, she said abruptly, "Didn't you hear? Oleg's dead!"

"What?! ...what happened?"

"He had a heart attack," she announced. His partner was running a pyramid scheme and fled the country with $25,000 and the police arrested Oleg saying he was responsible for the money. He had a heart attack on the spot and died. Wow.

A year or so later Dan ran into Tajir. He asked him how it was going. Dan said, "Business is still slow..." Tajir laughed and waved.

God deals strongly with those who mess with his own! Sometimes a lot sooner than we expect! If I grapple with fears (like death or the mafia) yet realize that there's Someone much more powerful than these, then I can work through smaller fears that keep me from living real life. Sometimes we don't even know what those fears are, but not identifying them keeps us in ruts and builds walls. First, I have to stop and identify the fear that is

4

trying to grab me and admit it and then begin taking it to the One we should fear above all. I needed that lesson! Raising a family in a foreign land can be a fearful thing. This was a beginning for me in dealing with my fears.

~for growth~

To start understanding yourself, identify a fear that may be holding you back.

What do you think you are most afraid of? Why?

What are the fears behind those fears?

Think it through. If your worst fear happens then what?

Can we go with God to our worst fears, face them, talk them through with him and let him speak to our spirits to break the power fear has in our lives?

"The eye of the Lord is on those who fear him...."
PSALM 33:18, ESV

Some names changed.

CHAPTER 2

MINING LOSS

"We must embrace pain and burn it as fuel for our journey."

Kenji Miyazawa

What we do with loss tells us much about who we think God is. I had a great fourth grade public school teacher, Mr. Ackerman. He was the camp-director type who had us all wash the classroom floor in an effort to teach us to work together. He took us on environmental walks in nature and taught us to cook a foil lunch over the campfire.

One ordinary day in the midst of a noisy class, he stopped, glared at my classmate, Arthur, stalked over to his desk and hoisted him up out of his seat taking him from the classroom out into the hall. His reason?

The young boy defiantly said a swear word. A seeming small matter today, but not then. That was one of the many little things that my teacher did that showed me something in him that was different. He was man enough to do something for a cause he thought was important. I needed to see that and it made me very curious. I had managed to uphold quite a reputation of popularity and ambition at age nine. After that year of school, I was gloating over my straight "A" report card outside on the patio as my family was eating dinner, enjoying the warmth of early summer. My Dad had gone in to answer the phone. When the sliding door opened again, he carefully stepped out. Then they came, these words, intruding my soul, as swift and stealth as a subterranean rift. He numbly announced that my three-year-old brother had just died.

"What?! Died...?" I silently protested.

He had a hole in the septum of his heart and had been in surgery.

Why didn't we know more about this? This was too abrupt. I didn't know it was that serious. I was so confused. I remember at times my little brother having an ashen blue tint and my mom being worried. Why didn't we talk about it more? Why wasn't any-one of us there with him? My heart was groping for answers... about life, about what this meant, about why people did or didn't do things. The rest is a swirl of haze. I remember though, going into my bedroom and yelling at the pink crucifix I had on my wall. That's the first spontaneous prayer I remember praying, if it was a prayer. I was mad. I had learned prayers at Catholic Church but they were memorized, not from me. This one was from me! "Why would you do this, God?"

Well, what did God have to do with it? I had never thought of him as that close, but when it came to death, I guess I thought he could be to blame. I silently wondered and waited not knowing how to react.

Even after Jody's death, I don't remember ever talking about it as a family. I do remember a lot of quiet suffering, nagging ques-tions and confusion, and sadly, I pushed all the questions to the back of my mind and carried on.

Years later, with a family of our own, we had another loss, miniscule in comparison to Jody, however, representative of many things. And by this time some things were coming to the front of my mind and layers of callous were being peeled off. When we arrived to work in our host country, our youngest child was eighteen months old. Within our first year we needed to procure a security system for our house. The way that was done in our adopted country was by buying a dog! So, Dan did some research and came bouncing home one day, telling the kids to look in his brief case (or broof case, as they said it) and there they found a little black ball of fur with brown markings. We all fell in love.

This sweet little vulnerable Rottweiler was to be our security system in this backward, unpredictable, foreign land! She grew in wisdom and stature, and in favor with us but not with any stranger. As she grew, her playful frolicking way turned into gruff throaty barks and growls when anyone unusual appeared. We put her behind a gate when visitors came into our house and they quickly learned the fear of Ayoo (her name meant "bear" in the local language). She was a playmate to our kids, a willing workhorse to tow their sleds, an alarm system at our front gate, a jogging companion in the mornings, a 'bouncer' of the next-door neighbor's chickens that came over the fence and a chaser of stray cats. She picnicked and camped with us. She heartily greeted us every day and one of Dan's playful sayings to the kids became, "who loves you?" They would say, "Ayoo!"

Twelve years after we brought her home, she started to slow down. Yet she still took us jogging religiously. We were looking at a move to another country and knew we were going to have to do something with her. Our family was at a different stage  and we were making some adjustments. As the months went by we noticed a growth on her belly and found the cancer was too far along to treat. She was suffering, so at the vet's advice, and with the kids' permission, we grievingly decided to put her to sleep. Well, in this country you bring the bag and bury the pet yourself. So, we did. I couldn't stay and watch while they put her to sleep. I left the concrete bleach-scented office, stepped out into the soggy remnants of winter and wept. When Dan finally came out carrying Ayoo in a bag, he was weeping too. We took her to a field in view of the majestic mountains, dug a hole and buried her. We didn't have a habit of crying much, unfortunately, but it came out in gushes that day. It was like we were saying goodbye to much more than just her. It was goodbye to our kids' childhood, goodbye to our 12 years in this fledgling country, goodbye to all that had become familiar, to a team of dedicated people, to watching our friends encounter truth that changed them, and goodbye to our hopes for this land that were yet unrealized. That experience made me curious. Why did it impact us so deeply?

Goodbyes are about loss; loss of familiarity, of the chance to make a difference, of hard-grown relationships as well as hoped-for relationships, and unfinished conversations.

Had there been much change because of our presence?

Loss is painful and causes numbness. Can we push through the numbness and see how our hearts were affected? Through experiencing the loss, what were the meaningful gains? One gain for me was my heart was changed.

Some gains we could see in our losses included:

- Recognizing the depth of the relationships that awakened grief
- Pondering the shallowness of other relationships
- Appreciating each other's labor and sacrifice
- Evaluating what went well, what didn't; gathering the lessons from mistakes and cultural blunders
- Realizing the joy of having adjusted to a new land and language
- Seeing how the upheaval of another move gave the

chance to reevaluate our lives and possessions, as well as our souls.

Loss opens our soul for re-evaluating. We can either follow it to the deepest part, take time to mourn and make some decisions; or we can close it up and let it fester. The process of dealing with loss can end in despair or eventually lead to gratitude and a new start. Loss can be a step toward change but we may need the help of others. If we just move on and don't grieve our losses, they can show up later, somewhere...in anger or depression, dysfunctions or physical illness.

~for growth~

When facing loss do you see a tendency in yourself that leads to numbness or pushing the soul aside?

Take time to think about your life. What have been your most painful losses?

Have you let yourself grieve those?

What does the fact that you remember those particular losses tell you about yourself? This is important to think about and process with someone.

Do you see any gains in your losses yet, any gifts in the pain?

Working on these inner issues will free up "RAM" in your inner being to move forward toward fuller life.

Write a lament. Here's one of mine:

After my father-in-law's memorial service, I contemplated the inevitable misses in life, the cries for help, the absences at crucial junctures, the lack of voice – what I wish I would've noticed, where

I wish I would have been, when I wish I could have listened better to someone or held my tongue. How drowning these thoughts can be! Yet how redeeming to know God is orchestrating me.

Now that I know, I go
To places in the past, I should have been
Noticing faces that needed a touch
Traces of sorrow unheeded, feelings ungreeted
Unspoken questions seeded
To grow into ogres of thought
That overshadow the truth that I sought
The love I fought
for you.
Heaves of hind-sighted regrets, finding
Way for an undiscovered voice;
"It's not as it should have been," yet spliced
With reaches both ways
Clarity and haze.
Stillness of time bidding me stay
But I cannot dwell in the powerful array
That holds me in its mire.
So, I fight for you & for me,
As I see in new light what is higher.

"...so you will not grieve like people who have no hope."
1 Thess. 4:13, NLT

CHAPTER 3

EMPTYING

"God has shot his arrow and made my heart his mark."
College band's paraphrase of Lamentations 3:12

At my suburban public middle-school, a teacher told me that with my grades and abilities, I could do whatever I wanted with my life. Wow... that can go to a thirteen-year-old's head! I was very involved in a nationally competing gymnastics team with the chance of moving up. Outwardly, I had what most girls my age wanted. But there

Photo - Tim Ross

was a yearning within, a questioning. Yet out of this middle-school milieu came an unexpected call, a wooing. I was caught up in, swept away by something else loosening my hold on temporal things. I had come across a community of people who did life together, who believed and loved God. They connected with each other in very practical, meaningful ways. I hadn't seen that before. This led to intense curiosity, adolescent soul searching, and a newfound faith that brought me purpose. I started on a different path, to the dismay of some people in my life. I was a teenager and I think I got a bit too radical. Things changed; I didn't have as many friends; I spent more time alone; I hung out with a fringe group and went inward a bit, probably too much.

Later in high school, the youth leader became my standard for life. He took seriously his charge to teach us, and this teaching put a longing in me for God and his Word. He was still in process too though and had issues he needed to resolve. Even so, I leaned on his faith. So much so, that when he had to resign due to compromises in his life, it hit me like a death. The same confusion I faced with my little brother's death revisited me with no one to walk me through it. I felt an empty silence, a lack of direction in how to deal with this. While many adults were relieved to get this unique man out of our midst, I grieved a gaping loss. They were doing what they knew was right, but there was little communication. I took it to the back burner, my default, giving me more to work on later. I hate non-communication, yet I'm very good at it.

So there I was - no longer who I was before I knew my youth leader, and not quite knowing who I was without him. To some degree he had become my identity. Now I needed to move beyond that phase of faith. I had been emptied of lesser loves, and needed filling with another Love. Fortunately, this young leader had given us a strong foundation of Truth to build on; I am forever grateful for that! But I was still crushed and floundering. Others in the youth group seemed to give up or just move on. Some got bitter, some felt victimized. I withdrew in my disillusionment. I knew there was hope, but it took a few years to struggle my way out of the cloud and find myself..

Years later I hit another disillusionment patch when we landed in a seemingly forsaken post-Soviet land, where Oleg (previously mentioned) entered our story. Prior to this assignment my husband and I had lived in Bolivia, South America for seven years where we learned the language and culture, had four kids, worked with a team of movers and shakers and had our share of adjustments.

Photo - Cheri Magarrell

Starting again in yet another unknown culture, and a stark one at that, I had nothing left to give. Though I wanted to be there, my heart wasn't yet. I wanted to want to learn the language, and I hoped to do something that would be of help to the people of this land where God had supposedly been dead for decades. This place seemed to be paused in century-old ways. Leftover Soviet concrete rubble and dilapidated pipes on display. Crumbling infrastructure alongside breathtaking scenery that no one seemed to notice... snow-capped mountains, blue mesmerizing lakes, jutting rock faces.

The dusty gold plastic amulet, with Arabic writing swinging from the rearview mirror of the taxi, added to the mishmash of cultures. Things were used and overused; overlooked and worn out, little shanty towns passed us; miles of stout, plastered brick, gingerbread-looking cottages lined up, smoking in the cold, fatigued haze. It was a long, frigid ride to our new home.

We arrived in the capital on a very dreary day in early September, 1994. There was nothing of beauty that I could find. Looking out of the third-floor apartment window, I saw the rusty, arthritic playground equipment, broken glass, and old crusty men in the courtyard. That's where my kids were supposed to play?

Though I hadn't admitted it to myself yet, I had in the back of my mind decided the language was too hard and I would thus stay at home and just take care of the kids, the house and my husband. That's about all I could muster up at the time. So, my first week there I went out to meet another expatriate woman with five kids, thinking I'd get some sympathy. When she opened the door, she was in the middle of her language lesson, her kids were working on their schooling and she mentioned something about going to help at a clinic.

I had some talking to do with the Lord about comparison, about copping out, about relying on myself, about his plan that didn't line up with mine. It's been a on-going discussion.

But I am finding that disillusionment, combined with emptying myself of (letting go of) what I thought would or should be, can lead to growth! Often facing disillusionment is the beginning of real faith. Or it can lead to a reactionary betrayal of faith; throwing out the baby with the bath water.

It was a long tunnel of questions about walking with God, and though I didn't have many answers I clung to what I still knew was true. It is amazing the power of our misconceptions and what it takes to break through them. Thankfully God is willing to go to great lengths to show us what we wrongfully believe about him and ourselves. I had ideas about God that needed reworking and ideas about myself that were a result of living in a fallen world. Free us, Lord, to really want the truth whether it fits into our boxes or not!

Truth is where the freedom is! At times God wounds, because he has to deal with stingy, proud, self-centered me. Not to condemn me but to free me! If I never see that I am proud, I won't see the need to be transformed. If I think God only cares for me when I am perfect, I will stress over not being perfect and never face truth.

We are fragmented... and fractions of ourselves and He's in the business of putting us together. This often happens through emptying us. This emptying isn't the Buddhist kind where you try to rid yourself of all desire (which strips us of our humanity) it is rather the kind that rids us of our boxes of limited thinking. God is always blowing out our boxes!

~for growth~

Have a soul conversation:

Learn to acknowledge and improve your self-talk. One way is to begin a list of underlying messages playing in your head, like "I'm on my own" or "I'm not worthy of any-one's love."

Where have you been disillusioned? Or felt misled by God? Why?

Have you gone there with God and His Word to lay it all out and listen?

Can you admit your disappointments to God? Or others?

"If your life is broken, it may be that the pieces will feed the world. The loaf will feed only a little boy."

Elizabeth Elliot

CHAPTER 4

FACING SELF

"You carry your culture with you—whether you're conscious of it or not. Until you see yourself as you really are, you'll see both yourself and others from a distorted point of view."
                Global Mission Handbook, Hoke and Taylor, p. 38

The excitement of going to high school was tangible; the crisp feel of the coming Pennsylvania fall energized me on my late August bike ride; the fun of football games with friends, new clothes and classes with older students. In the flurry of try-outs for field hockey, dance club, and chorus, I wanted to live out my faith. I was a bit timid and new with the things of faith, yet had a teenage surety that I knew what I wanted. But some things were still deeper in the want category than I was able to see; like the attention of that really cute 11th grade boy who asked me if I would let him copy my homework. I felt a twinge of guilt as I said, "Sure!" and got a chance to look into his gorgeous eyes as I shuffled around to get the paper. I failed that temptation....and felt deflated at how easily, but there would be more temptations to come, and this just gave me a glimpse into the truth about myself and what I really wanted.

Now that's the question. What do we really want?

Can we name it? Whether it's something we *should* want or not...

I don't think I thought about what I really wanted for a long time after that. So much of what we do is done without thinking. But as we grow and learn to think things through, we have to ask ourselves this question. Because if we can face the fact that what we really want is maybe not what we should want, then we're getting down to honesty and the possibility of change.

We raised our kids in a small post-Soviet city of 600,000 people where life closed down about 8pm. The options for entertainment were slim so our kids developed a keen imagination, making forts out of rubble, snow or furniture and finding fascination in the simple things of life. When we watched TV, Dan made a point to talk back to the vacuous commercials to foster in the kids a healthy suspicion for any coercion to get their attention, their money, or their heart. Any commercial, telling us what we wanted instead of letting us decide was a candidate for sarcasm. "Life will be much easier if..." "You need this to make you feel good." "New discoveries for easy weight loss". "Buy more, save more!" Yeah right. Who's kidding whom? It was a good exercise in dissecting our wants.

There are so many parts of ourselves we don't see. Our souls have great capacity for self-deceit. It takes a situation to help us see from another angle... a situation like a tough relationship or an unwanted circumstance where condemnation, anger, selfishness, jealousy and the like come bubbling to the surface. Too often we allow ourselves to justify or numb these inner reactions and "self" never gets faced or, we live in condemnation or denial. Any spouse or parent will tell you, if they're honest, about the new areas of needed growth they saw in themselves when they had to make room in their life for another voice.

When I clue in that something going on inside me is wrong, and finally allow it into my consciousness, then I have to do something with it or it will fester. If my contempt for another person is sneering at me, muddying my thoughts, I have some choices to make. I remember vividly the time a friend was telling a group of us about her wayward son. Immediately my thoughts leapt to condemnation (and almost satisfaction!) that he was reaping some of what he had sown. I caught myself, in alarm, hoping no one heard my thoughts and realized this thing was bigger than me. I had to face it.

That's the problem with sin. It's bigger than us. We can't deal with it on our own. If we want change there's got to be a turning from what we ourselves can bring to the situation, and a turning to what God can bring to it. It is his power over sin that we can bank on, not ours. The awesome thing is that when we experience that power, the change in us can surprise us. His forgiveness is instant but his work in us continues. As we work together with him until Christ is formed in us (Galatians 4:19) he actually transforms our hearts. I knew my heart had actually been changed when the next time I heard about that woman's son doing much better, I genuinely rejoiced.

When we catch ourselves looking down the wrong path with all its appeal and glitter; if we can just see beyond it; see it for the fraudulent appeal that it really is, we will sprint in the other direction. Proverb 4:27, NASB says, "Turn your foot from evil." You see, our foot goes toward evil without us trying. That's the norm. We need to *turn* it. The pull is dangerous, and its power much greater than us....is it any wonder we get trapped? Sin shouldn't so much surprise us as sadden us. A better choice could have been made.

Surely you have noticed the myriad temptations that pull you away from the truth about yourself, to escort you to comfort, ease, pleasure, escape... or despair. There is a time for comfort and pleasure for sure! But there is also a time to ask God to search us and know us and reveal the hurtful ways in us. Sometimes we need that healthy sarcasm to talk back to the temptations that come our way so we can break through and see the truth about ourselves.

"Our real idea of God may lie buried under the rubbish of conventional religious notions and may require an intelligent and vigorous search before it is finally unearthed and exposed for what it is. Only after an ordeal of painful self-probing are we likely to discover what we actually believe about God."

The Knowledge of the Holy, A.W. Tozer

~for growth~

Facing self is not an exercise in despair or condemnation; it takes us to freedom. For example, if I'm struggling with pride and can't seem to get beyond that, my pride can become the focus and begin to depress and defeat me. Freedom comes when I say, "Yep, I'm proud and I hate that and am sad about it", BUT

1. I am forgiven when I confess. This sin is fully paid for!
2. I have the power of Christ to free me from thinking too highly of myself.
3. I can say, "thank you God!" I don't have to sulk wishing I could be better. I can rather work with God as he seeks to transform me into His image. I can "wear forgiveness like a crown" as the song goes. There is great gain that comes from facing ourselves. God is gentle with us. That's such a soothing thing for our fragile hearts to know!

Do you notice the pull in your heart and mind toward hiding from the truth about yourself?

The enemy's tactics can be very subtle, especially for those who live outwardly clean lives. Examine your temptations, angers or worries. What do they tell you about yourself?

"The kingdom of self is heavily defended territory."

Eugene Peterson

CHAPTER 5

SHIFTING PARADIGMS
(paradigm – a generally accepted idea of how things work.)

*"You can be straight as a gun barrel theologically and as
empty as one spiritually."*

A. W. Tozer

New leaders and very green in overseas work, Dan and I were
joined by a team of young, promising volunteers on a mission
to the fertile Cochabamba valley of Bolivia's Andes Mountains in
1986. We'd had a good beginning there, having stayed with a gre-
garious Bolivian family who enveloped us in their family life - dirt
floors, chickens, foibles and all. The courtyard housed the only
bathroom for the whole extended family. The toilet was situated
almost under the shower so when you took a shower it got all wet.
The seat had one of those terry cloth sponge covers on it. It was
always soaked. I learned the squatting technique pretty quickly!
The redeeming factor was a sliced view of the snow-capped
mountains through the top of the metal bathroom door! Though
the accommodations were less than posh, the hospitality was five
star! A new paradigm of life!

After our initial period of language and culture learning we
were ready to lead the work. Our underlying concept of leadership

was conventional and workable but not sustainable for good relationships, or for the best results. We really didn't even know we had a concept of leadership, we just went on instinct. And that's the problem. We had prepared for many things as we embarked on a career overseas but leadership struggles and relationship issues were not at the top of the list. All the other things seemed more important. But relationship issues are often what make or break a team.

In his book, The Five Dysfunctions of a Team, Patrick Lencioni highlights the need for a foundation of trust upon which the other factors for team success can be built. And though our teammates were not pejorative, they began to manifest disgruntled attitudes... which we quickly dismissed in order to focus on the "important" things.

In our minds the mission was the goal and if they didn't like it, well...what were they doing here? We had work to do and urgent business to tend to, so petty concerns were not entertained. Of course we didn't say that, but the message got across. I noticed that conversation and creativity was strained and meetings were a bit of a drudgery. We pressed on, but something was missing.

By God's grace, we happened upon some masters-level leadership courses being offered and I was drawn to this training. Dan and I decided to enroll so we headed down to Santa Cruz, Bolivia on the bus to start two weeks of classes. On the way, we stopped at a roadside café and had about a half hour until the bus would be departing. Dan took his brief case in since it wasn't safe to leave it on the bus. We enjoyed the spicy roadside cuisine, got back on the bus and careened down the mountain roads of Central Bolivia as dusk settled on the passing guardrail-less cliff edges. After about 15 minutes Dan sat up, looked around and said, "Oh no...!" My heart sank. He had left the brief case at the café with our passports and all the money for our stay, tuition, and the trip back! He hurried up to the driver and asked if we could turn around. No way. They just don't do that. Dan said, "Well, just stop and let me off."

We had our three children with us and all of our luggage. He would have to walk or hitchhike back to the café and then find his way to us. This was before cell phones were part of our lives. So, I'm panicking, he's getting off the bus and after he is out of sight I remember that he had the address to where we were going to stay. All I remembered was the name of the guesthouse. So, I took a deep breath, shook my head, and called on God.

You learn, being married to an ambitious young world changer, where to go to get your strength and help.

Dan wasn't always there and that was ok... most of the time. It pushed me deeply to God. I could complain to him like David did in Psalm 142:2, ESV "I pour out my complaint before him..." I didn't know what I was going to do when three little kids and I arrived at the country's largest city, at night, with no directions or connections... but I knew God was there. It turned out that when we got off the bus into the balmy Santa Cruz breeze the first taxi driver I talked to 'happened' to know where the small guest house was and took us straight there! But I was worried and very skeptical about the money in the briefcase. This was rural Bolivia, the poorest nation in South America. What were the odds?

Meanwhile Dan hitched a ride in a truck back to the café, and scuttled in. The lady behind the counter recognized him immediately and triumphantly brandished his briefcase. He found it intact with everything in its place! Wow. Such relief. The Lord's angels on the job! Gotta love honest people.

After a brief celebration of appreciation to the workers, he had to find a way down to Santa Cruz. A truck with a tall load of cargo and a troop of peasants camped on top was preparing to leave the café. The drivers insisted he ride in the sleeper cab with them. He sat on the bed behind, between them. They offered him coca leaves, which they chewed non-stop the way American drivers drink coffee, and seemed to thoroughly enjoy hosting a foreigner to help pass the time. He made it to us after midnight with the good news, and it gave us a clear sense that God wanted us there and had something to say to us.

And He did. One of the courses we took was "Group and Conflict Dynamics". The professor stated his thesis at the beginning saying that if we use the job (the Great Commission) to develop the people we're working with, the job will get done in a more effective and fulfilling way and the people will grow, change and be energized. I knew this didn't sit well with Dan. Being quite task oriented he took seriously the job to which we were called, so he found it hard to believe this would really be the best way to get the job done. After all we weren't therapists focusing on people's issues. But session after session the professor gave evidence to support his thesis. He shared case studies - Jesus' with the Twelve, the time poured into them and his heart toward them. We did group exercises and role plays.

After two weeks we were sold on the concept and went back to our team to lay out our findings. God wasn't only using us to get his job done, but he was using the job to get us done! Immediately there was relief in the air! But it would take time to reformat our team culture. The way we had functioned wasn't going to change overnight. But a major shift had taken place in our minds. Paradigm shifts take faith, risk and humility. We remained equally serious about the job but sought to engage each person in a mode which better suited them and their talents, and which bound us together for a worthy cause. It was a beginning.

To the degree that you influence anyone, you are a leader. To lead like our Leader, Jesus leads takes paradigm shifts because it is counter to our natural ways. We need to reorient our minds... to let God shift us.

~for growth~

If you're tired of your ways and want to learn his, he says, "Take my yoke upon you and learn of me, for I am gentle and humble of heart." Matt. 11:29, NIV That's the all-powerful God of the universe talking! Reflect on what it means to be in the yoke with Him—learning.

CHAPTER 6

REMOVING LOGS

"Arise complacent women..." (and men!)

ISAIAH **32:9**, AUTHOR'S PARAPHRASE

The billowing American flag beckoned us into the sunny Miami airport, the very place we departed seven years earlier heading to Bolivia with only a few duffle bags and no kids. Returning, we had four kids, and a bundle of luggage along with kid paraphernalia. The seven years had been productive in some ways. The team we left behind was growing and our organization was merging into another. Dan was asked to help with the transition as well as propose the opening of another field.

Leaving was bittersweet as usual. There were new people joining the team with great experience, looking into innovative ways to reach one of the largest people groups in South America. We felt good about that, though sad to be leaving at a key time. There had been a bit of conflict on the way out that tainted the goodbyes; misunderstanding, miscommunication, feelings that things were not resolved.

We found a little temporary apartment in Florida, got our oldest into kindergarten and unpacked for a while. Living back in

America was a needed change. I felt scattered and bombarded, tired from packing, moving, travel, and unpacking, taking care of kids, concerned about their hearts; wondering about myself, disappointed in how we were relating as a family, wondering if our work was effective, missing sleep, dealing with feelings of distance or incongruence or hurriedness...noticing my readiness to point at things to blame or to look for someone whose specks I could remove... while I had logs.

> "How can you say to your brother 'Let me take the speck out of your eye and behold the log is in your own eye. First take the log out of your own eye and you will see clearly...'"
> MATTHEW 7:4, 5B, NASB

Complacency stalks us. We are lulled into comfort and we craft good reason for it. I'm not talking about God's wonderful, needed comfort. I'm talking about our own self-defined zones of what we will and will not do. Just as the women of Judah, who lived in the Lord's blessing, needed Isaiah's warning hundreds of years before Christ, so we need warning from being lured into smug self-preservation and stunted growth. It's the nature of us all to fade into ease. Isaiah speaks pretty bluntly to those who looked for their happiness and security in this life. They had all they wanted and so were blinded to their need for change. They abused their plenty. Prophet Isaiah's words, meant to stir them, were simply dismissed. They will have to answer to God, as we will, for how we used the life he gave us.

I can get comfortable with "logs in my eye," when I'm supposed to take them out. Taking them out is not an easy thing to do! We're used to having them in there and actually they can be nice to hide behind. Anyway, I don't want to spend so much time on myself. Look at everyone else's problems!

It seems one of the hardest things is to let God's Word work seriously on our hearts. Taking our logs out is what God says to do first, yet we would much rather work on others' specks. This is especially important for leaders. Though often neglected because of the "tyranny of the urgent", leadership of self empowers leadership of others.

Ruth H. Barton says it beautifully, "Spiritual leadership emerges from our willingness to stay involved with our own soul – that place where God's Spirit is at work, stirring up our deepest questions and longings to draw us deeper into relationship with him."

Joshua conquered, because the Lord fought for him.

JOSHUA 10:42.

We conquer our "logs" because He fights for us. It's both me and God. I conquer, the Lord fights. We engage exceeding difficult battles in prayer and in person and conquer evil because, and only because, God fights on our behalf.

Long, ordinary, mundane days are good for this. I need to find my way to the "closet" to get perspective and receive his word to my soul. This takes planning. In a church service we attended in our first few weeks in Florida, the speaker set forth a challenge. He said, "What is one thing you need to change right now to make a difference in your life?" I knew right away. I knew I had to start my early morning times with God again. This had been a habit for me, but four kids later, I was faltering. And the logs were building up. There were plenty of excuses I could've used, but I wanted change. And I knew what I needed to do. I had to make sure concentrated time with God was a priority.

Friends heading to the mission field wrote, having just found out they were pregnant, and said, "Jackie, I often think of your words to us one Sunday morning, telling us to not allow ourselves to get too comfortable. Well, we're NOT comfortable! But we're trusting God every wild step of the way. So thankful at least HE knows what he's doing!"

I said, "Welcome to the club!"

~for growth~

Can you distinguish between needed comfort and escape into a comfort zone?

Ask God (and a trusted friend) for insight into your logs.

CHAPTER 7

REVISITING THE PAST

"If our yesterdays are in a state of good repair, they provide strength for today. If not repaired, they create havoc."

A Resilient Life, Gordon McDonald

You've heard of a great man who said "Forgetting what is behind...I press on ..." Well, the only way we can forget our past is if we revisit it. If we don't go back and take a look and re-work the negative things in our early lives, our past remains with us, influencing all we think and do, whether we like it or not.

My father as a college student

Before the Bolshevik Revolution in 1917, a teen-aged girl in the Ukraine peering into the unknown, decided to brave the harrowing cross-ocean journey to an unknown life in an intimidating new world. What kind of courage... or desperation drives a decision like that?! She found work as a nanny, struggled to make it and eventually married a young Ukrainian man who, as the story goes, had come over on the same boat. They scraped together a life in the coal region of Pennsylvania where immigrants were settling. My father was the 10th of their 11 kids. He still uses his Ukrainian words at times and sings a folk song (that we could sparsely understand after we learned Russian) describing the monotony of life in the old world. The words went something like this:

Early Monday morning we go together to the field to plant the hay, early we go together.
Early Tuesday morning we go together to the field to cut the hay, early we go together.
Early Wednesday morning we go together to gather the hay....
Early Thursday morning we go together to bring in the hay...
Early Friday morning we go together to sell the hay...
Early Saturday we get paid and drink our money away...
Early Sunday morning we cry together, we cry all day....

His childhood was riddled with adventure and tragedy; diving off cliffs into gorges, unhealthy work in the coal mines, orthodox religion, and years of nagging want during The Great Depression and World War II. His father died of black lung disease when my dad was in eighth grade. Despite these adversities, he excelled in school and after being noticed by a high school math teacher was given a scholarship to go to college.

While at college he worked several jobs, studied like mad, fell in love, graduated and got married. They had six kids (I was the second). He tells us of a time when he and my mom were driving over a toll bridge and didn't even have a dime to get through. He had to turn around and go another way. He worked several odd jobs before landing one as a pharmaceutical salesman. After several lean years and a few tries he reapplied to medical school, was accepted and went on to become a doctor several grueling years later. That kind of story makes me love America! Where else could a poor family have the opportunity to do such a thing? I've lived in several countries where it is highly unlikely. He's an inspiration to me and I hope for half the determination and wonder in life that he has.

But you know, the old world is still in him. We joke about this and my mom just shakes her head. He has a hard time spending money; he saves things and finds every way he can to not have to buy things. He gloats about the fact that the running shoes he wears are twenty years old and they were secondhand when he got them! He has a hard time with gifts. He will never turn on the a/c, even in the stifling days of summer. My poor mom. This can be very annoying but it shows his past is still with him.

Somehow the idea of his obituary came up in a conversation and he said, "Don't pay for that, just say, "Joe died." My sister said, "But you get five words free." My Dad, after a moment of contemplation, came back with, "Ok say, 'Joe died. Car for sale.'" The laughter took a while to die down. We call him Poppy now and he's adored by his grandchildren.

I don't know all that was left in the back of his mind, but I know some of it was passed on to me; his ways of relating, his philosophy of life and views of others; some good, some not. I think everyone has to come to the place of forgiveness for their parents, no matter how bad, average, good or wonderful they were. They cannot be all we wanted or needed them to be, nor were their parents for them, nor are we for our kids. We are all flawed. Counselor Dr. Larry Crabb says, "Parents are the first people every child turns to for what only God can provide. It's in that relationship that disappointment is deepest." And perhaps that is *so that* we will turn to God in this fallen, broken world.

It's a common thing when one turns forty or fifty to think about one's past. I started a few years before that. When I finally realized my life wasn't going to be what I had hoped it would be and began dealing with the disappointment, I was able to start working on things that came up in my heart one at a time.

So, I began letting my heart ask questions I didn't know were there. Questions like:

Why doesn't God just make it clear to me how best to help people here? Why is it so difficult?

If I've given everything and spent my life preparing for this why is it not coming together?

We live in a place of desperate need all around us. How do I fit into all this?

Is my understanding of God my own making? How have I misunderstood Him? Has he misled me? Who has He really made me to be?

I thought I understood who I was in my own culture; but who am I here? I don't fit. Why am I so exhausted? Is this overseas life going to mess up our kids? How can I take care of myself and keep up with everything else without going overboard? How can I keep myself sane in such a depressing place? What is spirituality? Is all of this worth it?

A lot of these questions were due to culture stress and a major geographical move. Deep things often come to the surface in high-stress situations. God orchestrates these moments to pull us close and transform us. I was ripe for some transformation.

As much as I could with four small kids, I spent time alone praying, reading and defining the things that had a grip on me. I remember in this time of quandary desiring to be part of a particular group of women. When I wasn't invited to something they were all doing, I felt overlooked, discarded. As I worked through this, I felt as though God said to me, "I know that pain. There are a lot of things I'm not invited to." This began to show me that my heart was set on something above Him. The sweetness of His presence in a painful moment was redeeming. That's what He's about, bringing us up out of our past, our ruts and the things that hold our hearts, into His purposes. He knows the damage it does to our hearts if they are set on anything over their Creator. This took me to a deeper look at my own past and how I arrived at some of my misguided conclusions.

Often, we get stuck in our spiritual lives because of things we hold on to or decisions our hearts made beneath our con-sciousness. In an Adult Development class in graduate school the professor said "Pass it back or pass it on." That is, if we don't deal with our stuff it'll get passed onto our kids (or others we influence) without us even knowing. That gave motivation to work on this area even though it would take breaking the inertia in my soul!

~for growth~

There are so many helps today for working on ourselves. And the process is actually sometimes the best thing we can do for others. God wants to work with us on us.

What questions is your heart trying to ask you?

Have you taken a look at the foundations of your past?

"It is always true to some extent that we make our images of God. It is even truer that our image of God makes us. Eventually we become like the God we image. One of the most beautiful fruits of knowing the God of Jesus is a compassionate attitude towards ourselves... This is why Scripture attaches such importance to knowing God. Healing our image of God heals our image of ourselves."

Brennan Manning

CHAPTER 8

STANDING ON SHOULDERS

"External change is inevitable, but internal change is a
choice. Make the choice to trust God in your adversity.
Don't seek quick fixes from God; seek Him!"

<u>Learning to Soar</u>, M. Willis

I'm intrigued with those who overcome odds against them to make strides of growth and change; intrigued because it usually takes something big, something out of the ordinary to lift them and make a difference. It takes a very conscious choice. And

Photo - Ariana Scott

that takes work on their part, cooperation over a period of time to work toward a greater goal. Like the flower that almost wishes the crack in the sidewalk into being, is the one who so desires a different way, they seem to find that crack or maybe cause it.

The oldest of five, my mom grew up in hometown USA where her family held together until tragedy struck. Her mother seemed to give up on life when her husband had an accident, which put

37

him out of work and into the bottle. He never recovered and thus the depression and lack of connection at home. Being the oldest, my mom was quite industrious, always finding work and ways to be with friends. I think she had some great friends. She talks some about faith, about angels and how she was kept from things and given so much help. She loved life then as she does now and had a resilience that seemed to say, "Sidewalk, I know you'd like to squelch any hope of me coming up through and blossoming and seeing life but you don't scare me and I'm not stopping." Ever the optimist, she pushed through and made a way in life. She didn't have the money to go to college but she worked on a campus and found favor by her skill and sharpness. And met the man. ☺ But he was Catholic, and she was Protestant, so no one came to the wedding. It wasn't a big deal, just a few friends and the priest, she says.

It was two very different cultures joining and though both had grown up in America they had very different outlooks. I don't think they knew what they were getting themselves into. But, they stayed together. I thank them for that! It would've been easy to give it up, walk away...well maybe not easy, but very tempting. She was strong and did everything around the house. My brother, sisters and I laugh about memories of her being up on the roof cleaning out rain gutters or power washing the patio. I don't think I ever saw her cry. I'm sure she did, but we didn't see it. She was resilient, having learned as a young girl how to survive.

She was the one home with the kids during Dad's medical school, and then later with more kids during residency and internship. I don't know what her hopes and disappointments were then, but she was there for us. She raised us and did what she knew. We always had a good meal, she made Christmas special for us, she taught us housework. And she learned to take good care of herself - probably the main thing that kept her healthy. I do love that about her. She's fun and fresh and played tennis into her eighties! She reads books and follows politics much more than I do. When I want to give up exercising or trying to look decent, I think of her and get my running shoes on.

I pray for the same amount of overcoming energy my mom has so I can continue working and living out what I have come to cherish as real life. I stand on her shoulders and hopefully my daughter (and sons!) can rise even higher as she stands on mine. Could she get closer to what we were meant to be; closer to breaking negative patterns of the past, closer to seeking deep genuine change as she lives her life on earth for others and for the sake of her Creator and Redeemer?!

We tend to become what we experienced. But when someone breaks that cycle it stands out as noteworthy. I'm meeting a lot of these people, who have taken responsibility for their lives and decided to change courses.

They are like the famous orphan, living as an alien in a foreign land, adopted by a relative, then taken from him to serve in the government. She rose to a high position and then realized her precarious situation when her boss decided those of her ethnicity should be annihilated. Though her first reaction was to hide, at the prompting of the one who raised her, she took time to think and pray and got Strength, and the right finesse to face her boss and her enemy... and redeem a whole nation. It came down to one woman making a very difficult choice. I met her in a Book. You've probably heard of her - Esther, Jewish queen of Persia in 480 B.C.!

When we get a sense of history, a sense of being a small part of the vast flow of people who have tread this earth, we are humbled into seeing that our struggles are very much like those who went before us; perhaps easier, perhaps not. They responded to life, to good and bad, to disappointment and doubt, to tragedy and success... and to God. Those responses marked their lives. Can we judiciously differentiate between what we want to imitate and what we want to change?

What do we want our lives to say when we're gone? Our choice may make or break those who follow us in the next generation. Are we building shoulders for them to stand on or making it hard for them to get a leg up? (Our life is not just about OUR life!)

~for growth~

How like or unlike those in your past do you want to be?

What are you going to say to the sidewalk trying to squelch you?

CHAPTER 9

CLUING IN TO CULTURE

"The Lawd do help da simple..."
AUTHOR'S PARAPHRASE OF Ps 116:6

When we head into another culture to live among the local people, our hope is to understand them... at least enough to become someone they will listen to. But the reality is we are clueless, especially when their culture is very different from ours. It's good to recognize that. It's where we have to start. After all, we're the guests in their country. When they look at us like we're from Mars because they can't understand a word we're attempting to say in their language, we need to just laugh at ourselves with them. But that means getting over any feelings of self-importance. And that was time consuming and exhausting for me. I thought I was pretty important. ☺

In his book, <u>Cross-Cultural Servanthood</u>, Duane Elmer offers perspective on what it means to serve someone in another culture. He suggests six steps: openness, acceptance, trust, learning, understanding, and serving. But it's easier to rush into someone's world, do what we think they need most, feel good about ourselves and our sacrifice; then rush home possibly having done more damage than good. So, our first years in Central Asia were largely about being close enough to people to learn about them and build trust so that our serving could be mutual and meaningful.

We shared a courtyard with a young local family. The house was small with two stories and two bedrooms. Our four kids were in bunkbeds in one bedroom. The small yard was a Godsend for our energetic family, especially when the alternative was a playground strewn with broken glass and frequented by questionable characters. This yard was a combination of driveway, garden, dog pen, storage and a place to dry clothes, but it offered ample opportunities for our kids to play.

One day, Zoya, the young wife across the yard was over and we talked about our kids. Happy that I was finally getting along in Russian, I asked if she thought she would have another child since she had only one little boy the same age as our youngest. She flippantly answered, "Oh, I've already thrown away so many." I looked at her hoping I misunderstood. But I knew that word – the one that was used when you throw away garbage.

It was like a pierce. There was no sign of conscience or concern that this practice might be wrong. In the Soviet times it was their method of birth control. They knew nothing else. At that moment I realized I was much farther from understanding them than I even thought. I had so much to learn about the core of their beliefs.

We would always be anomalies to them. Somehow though, it didn't keep us from loving them or them from loving us... or from wanting to hear why we came and what kept us there. They were so hungry for meaning, but trapped in a convoluted belief system that denied God; and at the same time, they struggled to cope with devious spirits.

Whatever we've grown up with that has a negative binding affect on us needs to be unraveled so we can see Truth. This journey may take years or can unravel in a moment.

Another of our Soviet friends came to realize as she considered faith that she readily accepted axioms or "givens" in math. An axiom in mathematics logic is a basic proposition of a system that, although unproven, is used to prove the other propositions in the system. This logic is what is used in any belief system. Once she accepted God as the "given," she was free to really believe him. And her life was lifted!

Becoming part of a different country takes you far from your old world. You are challenged and changed beyond anything you expected. Then when you head back into your home culture you feel clueless all over again, even at times like a social martyr; always a stranger, an anomaly. Some cross-cultural workers face this more than others. Though I love our times in our home culture, there's an underlying feeling of "it's not mine anymore." So, we're an anomaly here and an anomaly there. Where's our home? That is a struggle and even more so for our kids.

But I find comfort in Hebrews 11 where it actually says "God was not ashamed to be called their God..." because they were looking for a heavenly city. Their hope was in a heavenly home. I find myself wrestling with this regularly. I'm working on putting my hope in a heavenly home while using my earthly home for heavenly purposes!

~for growth~

How about you, how are you doing at understanding people unlike you?

In what place are you setting your hope... or rooting your sense of belonging?

As you seek hard after God there may be roots or props you're relying on that He needs to remove to strengthen your foundation in him. Are you ready and willing for that?

"This momentary light affliction is producing for us something eternal!"

2 CORINTHIANS 4:17, AUTHOR'S PARAPHRASE

CHAPTER 10

SLOW GOING

"This is the only time in history when I get to fight for God. Once I die...I'll be in celebration mode...this is my limited window of opportunity."

Joni Erickson Tada

The windshield wipers flung the downpour away as my mom held tightly to the steering wheel on an early morning rush to Philadelphia the summer of 1978. I tried to blink the puff out of my eyes. I had made a last-minute decision to go to nursing school, succumbing to my parents' desire that I get a practical degree that would give me a job. It wasn't my first choice, but I had concluded that it was the right choice for then. My mom's resilience in her responses to her stubborn daughter baffled me when I got far enough from the situation to see it. She'd made phone calls, found documents, and scrambled to help get me registered for a test to apply for nursing school. I didn't deserve her. Her patience toward me was steady and strong like the rain that morning. We made it on time and I passed the test.

In my very young days of faith I built quite a wall between my parents and me. They represented what I didn't want. Though this was naïve and immature, I was convinced God and I were on good terms and I didn't really need my parents. Though I didn't see it, my self-righteousness bull-dozed over them. I severed my ties emotionally, feeling I was following God. As far as I understood, I was - even though my attitude was passive aggressive at times -to make sure they knew where I stood.

God accepts us where we are. I can't change those days or my unfortunate adolescent reactions, and I think God has helped my parents forgive me and see some good in it. But the anguish I caused them saddens me. It was all part of my formation and figuring out who I was with God in my life. Over the years our relationship has repaired. I love to be with them now. I've learned a lot from them and owe them much. They are hardy, resilient people who have endured much harder things in their lives than dealing with haughty, self-important teenagers.

Spiritual pride was one of the things Jesus dealt with most harshly while he was on earth. It's a base sin that I had to begin asking Him to root out. Seems slow going! Our hearts lean a certain way and they need to be trained to change. Training takes practice. Practice takes time, patience and planning. If our growth seems slow maybe we need more practice. Our Coach brings things into our lives for that very purpose.

"...the mature, who because of practice have their senses trained to discern good and evil."

HEBREWS 5:14, NASB

"...no discipline is enjoyable...but afterward there's a harvest of right living for those who are trained..."

HEBREWS 12:11, NLT

Our second son, Bradley, called us from Penn State University and told us about how he was trying to find a way to talk with someone. He said, "I think I'm more like Mom; she feels like she's bothering someone when she talks with them, but Dad thinks he's the blessing of their day!" ☺ We laugh and are amazed at how we're wired because of differing scripts we live by and we have to ask, again, what are you saying God, here, now, in this stage? Never can we stop learning and growing, though we feel we should be so much farther along. Jesus said to some of his followers, "You are...slow of heart to believe." I feel I am often there, slow of heart. I need such work on my heart.

Like a good coach... God pushes us to train us. Even though it can be jolting, we move a lot farther faster if we submit to his training. How's your training going?

~for growth~

Spend at least ten minutes silent before your God and let him lift you by his truth.

Make a life journey line, plotting the highs and lows of your life. Look for places you should revisit to go deeper with Him. (It is helpful to do this with others, sharing and discussing as you go.)

List anxieties and translate into prayer; cast them on God; visualize His hands taking them. (My journey groups, mentioned in the last chapter, focus on these things.)

Turn the annoyance of adverse circumstances to a chance to overcome and look at the good. Even in small things – as they are good practice for the bigger things.

Arrest any disgust with people, process with God and let

him replace these with his concern, forgiveness or a word of care.

Relinquish the desire to defend self or blame someone else, and rather receive counsel and give grace.

Begin uncovering your "self-talk" deciphering what's behind it.

Memorize verses that your soul needs.

These practices help us wade through our cluttered souls to discover those places where we are stuck. I have a friend whose flooded basement turned into a marvelous analogy. Her basement full of treasured savings, shelves of hoarded future useful-ness, flooded after a terrible storm, amounting to dreadful and expensive loss. The task of wading through it all was daunting, exhausting and... revealing. She came face-to-face with the truth about all her stuff. What was it saying to her? As she began unclut-tering her basement, she began uncluttering her soul, realizing she had staked much of her security in hoarding. This put her on the path to listening and freedom – and eventually gratitude for a flooded basement now transformed!

Fighting for God (letting him reign in us) starts in our own hearts. His rebukes realign us with truth that sets us free.

CHAPTER 11

DISSECTING THANKFULNESS

"Joy is always a function of gratitude — and gratitude is always a function of perspective."

Ann Voscamp

O ur first week in the former Soviet Union was a steep learning curve. We were in an apartment trying to bring some order to life with our four small kids in an unfriendly, foreign land. We were exhausted from the over thirty-hour trip to the other side of the world. Our sleep was messed up, we were figuring out where to get groceries; I had to learn to heat the milk to pasteurize it and I didn't know you needed to get stones out of the rice.

One learns when in a transition that the fewer changes you have to make at one time, the better. A person's system can only handle so much change at once. Well, our change 'barometer' was heading toward the red zone, if not there already. Dan had broken his front tooth on a little stone that was in the rice I cooked, so we were scrambling to find a dentist that we could trust in a place where we didn't yet speak the language or understand the system. As we were working on that in our jet-lagged state, I asked Dan to pick up some toilet paper when he went out, while I tried to

49

figure out how I was going to comb our three-year-old daughter's sweet, long, blonde hair which got badly tangled in the flurry. She was not cooperating; I was low on patience. We ended up going to get her hair cut.

Also our youngest was eighteen months old. This was in the days before disposable diapers had come to Central Asia. We were using cloth and didn't yet have a washer. We did have a bathtub though and I'll spare you the details.

When Dan got back he didn't have any toilet paper. He'd been all over town trying to look for it among other things and found none. Though we hated to, we asked our Australian neighbors if we could "borrow" a roll, and they were gracious. Now our daughter had to go potty, so she got ahold of the roll of TP (there was no little holder to put it in) and here's where "Murphy's law" kicks in. Never before this day had she dropped a roll of TP and never since then has she dropped a roll. But this day when there's quite a lack of TP to be found in the city; this day when we already have enough stressors to go around, enough exhaustion to put us under and enough newness to throw us off, she dropped our newly borrowed roll of toilet paper into the toilet...plop.... Woops. Ugh...

Eventually, I had to laugh...at least she hadn't gone potty yet. The toilet water was "clean" so we fished the sopping roll out and started unraveling it to hang it on the shower curtain rod. We learned how to use newspaper in the bathroom that day. Thankful?! I probably was not, right at that moment but I do have a photo of my darling little girl with her new hair cut standing by the swaths of TP hanging on the shower curtain rod. And she's smiling! So maybe I chose to thank God because, hey, at least we had a toilet! ☺

What's the big deal about being thankful? What difference really does it make? Does saying thanks or having gratitude significantly change anything? There's got to be more to it than an outward courteous gesture, because our Creator takes it very seriously. So much so that he says things like "For although they knew God...they did not give thanks to him, but they became futile in their thinking...and God gave them up to impurity and dishonoring of their bodies." Romans 1:21, 24, ESV. Somehow the attitude of thankfulness is foundational to understanding who we are.

"Offer to God a sacrifice of thanks giving and perform your vows to the Most High. The one who offers thanks giving as his sacrifice glorifies me."

PSALM 50:14, 23, ESV

It seems from this verse, that in our serving and sacrificing, God is very interested in our heart. He's not saying the sacrifices we make are worthless; it's just the way we're going about it is often lacking. For any sacrifice I make, if my heart is not in it, or if I do it only as a ritual or begrudgingly, it's apparently not glorifying to God; even if it inconveniences me greatly and I do it all by the book.

"Stop bringing your meaningless offerings..."

ISAIAH 1:13, NLT

Serving God overseas, or spending hours caring for a relative, or counseling, or giving of my time volunteering... it is surprisingly unimpressive to God unless combined with a heart of gratitude. He owes us nothing. And even after all we give, we owe him everything.

If we offer thankfulness and even choose to embrace the things in our lives that we're not thrilled about, it says something to God about our trust. It is costly to move or carry our non-acceptance of a situation to the front of our brain and acknowledge it honestly; to acknowledge how we feel about our health, our marriage or singleness, our kids or lack of kids, our neighbors, our finances, our job or whatever... and then to offer thanks. It costs to "embrace the dread". Or as an elderly friend used to say, to "accept the situation and praise God!"

What does it say to God when we do that? It's admitting that I'm not above being inconvenienced or interrupted and it's believing that he is aware of it and may be working in me through it. (He may have even arranged it!) It says, I'm not beyond needing help, It says, I'm not beyond dealing with my attitude. For example, toward the guy driving rashly in front of me. He may be foolish, but that doesn't have to affect my day or my attitude. Life is way too short to give ourselves to these lesser things. Working at being thankful means, "He's God and I'm not". It means my agenda is not necessarily top priority and, though it feels like it should be, I can bow to him believing that he is way above this situation and could change it in a minute but hasn't and for good reason. I can always ask for change but maybe he is trying to get my ear to hear what he's saying to me.

Murphy's Law was made for us to practice thankfulness. ☺ Fred R. Shapiro, editor of the Yale Book of Quotations said: "Murphy's law or the fourth law of thermodynamics" states: "If anything can go wrong, it will." The truth is we live in a messed up, fallen world so Murphy's law sometimes feels like the norm.

Day in and day out it's the little things that get to us, tempting us to whine. And I'm convinced it's a ploy against our well-being. I find myself wallowing there until I finally clue in that I don't have to stay there, feeling sorry for myself.

The reasons seem plausible enough, but am I missing the point? God may have "appointed a plant" or a worm, or a wind as he did for Jonah. "God appointed a worm..." Jonah 4:7, NASB God appoints things to get to us... to stop us (or interrupt us) to get our ear. How many times he says, "Listen, listen carefully, hear, give ear," but we're too occupied.

Jonah was fed up. He'd obeyed; done the thing God had asked of him. It was a dangerous task and getting there had been traumatic. And then what he feared would happen happened. The pagan enemies he'd been sent to warn repented and avoided the judgment he wished upon them. Jonah was not happy.

But God is so much bigger than all our pouting. More than just getting Jonah to do his work, he was using his work to get through to Jonah. He's trying to start a conversation with him and Jonah's not listening or really caring what might be on God's heart. He's done his duty and now he's ready to punch the time clock and go home. But God wants a conversation. It intrigues me that God ends that little book of the Bible with a tender question, to lift Jonah's eyes above himself and his own comfort. God cared deeply about the wicked nation that Jonah had no mercy for, and even about their cattle!

God is so beyond what we see and understand. Anything can be a pawn that He uses to help us grow. He uses even the worms! Do I believe that? Well, sometimes. But it's beyond what I can really grasp. We say with our mouths that God is in control, just as Jonah declared when God answered his prayer in the belly of the fish. But so quickly he fell back into the "how's this good for me?" category. Not that that's a bad question... unless the underlying accusation is, "God is not thinking about me." And in that case, it is giving in to a belief that He is not for me but rather against me... or maybe indifferent. And that is way wrong. That's where we get off track.

Now I'm all for complaining. Not the whiney "I want my way" kind. But the kind we do respectfully before God, like King David did, though he didn't always sound respectful. I think it really helps us process. We begin to see our real motives when we can "make our complaint before him" Psalm 142:2, ESV. Complaining is a privilege and a luxury though and can easily trap us if we don't take it to him. So, as we do this holy complaining, let's listen for the questions that God may be asking us!

~for growth~

What complaints most easily capture you?

How can you take your complaint to God?

CHAPTER 12

WORSHIPPING IN WANT

"What do we have that we have not received?"
1 CORINTHIANS 4:7, NASB

We were living in Thailand where three Buddhist monks walked down our little street occasionally to do their chanting for anyone who has their alms set out for them to take. This is what they live on. The chant is always the same eerie, crescendo-ing groan. I would peek out and try to grasp the scene. There is no communication, no care shown, as we know it, no talking, no expression, no assurance, hope or relationship that I could see. But the people bow with pleading looks, facedown enduring the ritual, then dutifully get up, put away the table that held their gifts as the monks walk off silently. It takes about 2 minutes. That's really what we as humans deserve for a god. One that is obscure, distant, capricious and unknowable. "They are made by human hands. They have eyes but cannot see, ears but cannot hear. Those who worship them will be like them." Psalm 115:5,6, 8, NIV Maybe people succumb to this because they know they really don't deserve more than that.

A Buddhist shrine near where we lived

But the God above all gods wanted more for us, more than we deserve, and saw fit to make that possible. Is that not just the most wonderful thing in the world!? The fact that He still wants to be our God is all gift. Anything we have or don't is gift. The difficulty, the pain, the nagging, the beauty, the joy, the amazement is gift to point us to him. The sooner we can embrace this fact the faster we can move on with Him.

In Thornton Wilder's play "Our Town," the Stage Manager guides the play, describing the locations and making key observations about the world the play creates. Occasionally throughout the play the actors freeze in time and the situation or mood is pondered. And the silent audience is moved by the moment, like when you push the pause button wanting to talk about what's going on in a movie. We so need those pondering moments where we take a look at what's in our hearts, underneath the surface. What subconscious habits of entitlement compromise our relationships? What selfish moods or discontented attitudes belie the reality that we are undeserving of all that has been given to us?

I remember a moment like this at a fledgling post-Soviet church we visited. They had just managed to put together a make-shift shelter in which to meet but the roof wasn't all it needed to be. On a rainy Sunday we had to keep our umbrellas up inside the new building. The budding worship team belted out twangy praises and we thanked the God who gives.

If we give attention, life is full of transcendent moments. What do we have that we have not received?

Lord, we are hushed...

by how you stoop to frailty, to the pettiness of our lives
by how your bigness encompasses the miniscule and astounds us
by how your timelessness lifts passing, insignificant moments to places of honor and change.
by how your mighty power takes on the tedious, common and weak and sweeps us off the thrones of our hearts and...we are hushed.

Transcendent moments are like winks from our Creator. Another one happened at a wedding...

Transcendence and Plastic Forks

There was something so rich and sweet about this joining of lives. The God-given glorious day, the mystery of the old stone buildings, the beauty of the common; daisies, black-eyed Susans, bare feet, and plastic forks. I think there was a godly awe among us at the picture of our Lord—beyond our grasp, yet so "among us and common" we could look right past it if not attentive. And the music - the joy of it, the fun, the creative melding of unique and classic instruments. The moving opus written and played by the groom as he watched his lovely bride come toward him down the grass aisle.

Solemnity and informality mingled in the pastor's words and

demeanor as he led the ceremony...so like Jesus. And we struggled with her father as he tried to express the difficult joy of giving away his daughter. The freedom of the bride and groom to abandon themselves to God and one another showed, expressed in their vows. What a great occasion for celebration and awe. What an amazing God to honor us with such beauty.

~for growth~

Pause and notice something today that you would usually pass by.

What do you learn?

Can you worship in want?

CHAPTER 13

GOING AFTER GREAT

"He stoops to make me great..."
2 SAM. 22:36, NIV FOOTNOTE

Kathy was intrigued with sign language and learned it in high school, feeling drawn to the silent symphony of lives intermingled because of a hearing condition. Moving overseas, she went so far as to learn Russian sign language meeting person after broken person in this struggling sub-culture. They began gathering to hear from her of the One who opens ears, physical ears at times and more importantly soul ears! Her deep care for them and immersion into their world made them listen. She took into her home two orphan teenaged girls and battled together with them for their souls and for freedom from a dejected past.

She walked beside those that society threw away. She gave up her job and the comfort of her homeland and found joy in helping them find their way in a world that shut them out. In her home I sat watching the silent conversation, the painstaking care with which she nurtured her "girls", helping them with schoolwork and teaching life skills that would lift their existence. I saw her skillfully help a small group learn to hear from God for themselves. I would call her great. Greatness comes in many varieties.

The following was written by Tassia, a photographer after a family photo shoot in May of 2012. It was the only weekend all six in our family were together in about a year, and we were celebrating our daughter's twenty first birthday.

Our family has plenty of struggles but we decided early to follow hard after God and he's making something beautiful "...for the display of his splendor." Isaiah 61:3b, NIV

Photo - Tassia Schreiner

"I think it is fair to say I have developed a crush on this family. As I watched them pile out of the van at Lockridge Park, I felt a rare timidity creep up within me knowing that I was in the presence of greatness. After spending a good portion of their life with young children in Central Asia, they moved to East Asia in an oversight role. Now that their children are grown up, their family is scattered across the globe. They are busy living out the abundance of Christ that finding them all together comes but once a year. The hour that I got to spend with them was truly blessed. I barely scratched the surface of getting to know their adventurous souls, and yet there is a good portion of my heart that is ready to up and move our family overseas to glean from Dan and Jackie's passion for life and God, and each other. The love I see through the lens at engagement sessions, as sweet as it is, doesn't hold a candle to the passion I saw in their eyes for each other and the mission God has called them to together. It was amazing to see a family, each member so full of love and life, so free, so aware of who they are in Christ."

Any greatness she saw was God's greatness in us. He is in the process of changing us and rearranging us. We are working through our dysfunctions like all families. Broken vessels with his glory shining through.

But I want to be great. I do! I want to have something to "show" for all these years on this earth! (Paul said, "In Christ...I have reason to be proud of my work for God" Romans 15:17, ESV.) I tend to measure that by certain things in my life and you probably do by other things in yours. Would you say (if no one were listening) that you are great? Do you want to be? Is that wrong?! Is it pride? Well, the One who is our example said, "Whoever wants to be great..." do this, Mark 10:43, NIV.

Of course, Jesus was talking about greatness in the kingdom of God, the kind of greatness that will last beyond this life, bringing something of value into the next life. Our measure is very different from God's, so if we can learn to want his kind of greatness, we do well. Clearly there is reward for that kind of greatness! (Hebrews 11:26)

~for growth~

How do you measure greatness?

How did Jesus measure greatness in Mark 10:43?

What kind of great do you want to be?

CHAPTER 14

VAPORIZING

"Yet you do not know what tomorrow will bring - what your life will be! For you are like a vapor that appears for a little while."

JAMES 4:14, CSB

Jogging past a graveyard on a lazy summer morning back in the U.S., thinking about what the day held, I tried to decipher what was worth worrying about. The morning was a bit misty and the graves were to my left, stadium-like and quite obtrusive on a hill facing me, staring. As I passed I imagined I was being watched, examined and spoken to. It was a bit disturbing. What might they say?! How many of them even had the privilege to take the time to be by themselves and jog? How did they spend their lives and were they glad? What would they do differently if they could? What would they say to me?

Can we ever get our heads around the idea that our lives are so short? Those feelings of, "where did that week of vacation go?" That longing to suspend the moments, the talks, the sweet looks, the lingering, the dialog. I often want to go back and say something else or not say it. I want a chance to embrace more of what's going on and enter in or bow out more gracefully. There's always too much for us to take in, in a day. That's the vapor...it's there, you hardly see it, and then it's gone.

To give an idea of this concept in teaching, I draw a line extending from wall to wall and put an arrow at both ends showing it's a never-ending line. Then I put a dot in the middle and ask what that is. The line is eternity... the dot my life. Though this analogy is insufficient to convey *"eternity"*, it helps show how short life is and that most people fail to grasp that this life is mostly not about this life. It's about the next life. It's about how we're going to affect things way beyond us. It's about transcending to the greater reality of the Creator God who is there. And we can influence that greater reality here in this realm. Now that's cool. Because as awesome as this life is, the next one is beyond better.

Why do we not live according to that? It seems so simple. But it's not. Our hearts get fickle, anxious, greedy, tangled and weighed down and we just don't really believe that the next life is much more important. If you want to know what you really believe (not what you say you believe) look at what you're living for. What are you most anxious about? What do you think about most? Ahha! We're caught by our thoughts.

Unchecked, my mind will go on thinking in earthly terms clouded with the temporary, self-justification, self-pity, self-condemnation, self-preservation and a lot more "self-sins" that keep our worlds squeezed down small. It takes some work to get our temporary perspective realigned and reoriented. That's why we need the Son. And the sun...

When my little sister would ask my Dad some cosmic question he would hold out his hand in a fist and say "Here's the sun..." trying to reenact a solar system to explain how the moon orbited or how the earth revolved. So now when we're trying to explain something to each other, my sisters and I put our fist out and say "Here's the sun..." ☺

God does that when talking about the cloud of witnesses "watching us" like the graves seemed to be watching me that morning. He says, you're tempted to lesser things, but consider this, look here, "Here's the Son."

"...since we are surrounded by so great a cloud of witnesses, let us lay aside every weight and sin which clings...let us run the race set before us looking to Jesus...consider him who endured such hostility..."Hebrew 12:1-3, ESV

~for growth~

What was Jesus' focus? How did he respond to life's unfairness and dysfunction?

How can I follow that example in today's world?

What's one thing I could lay aside in my life to open up more space for growth?

CHAPTER 15

LIVING BEYOND SELF

In our travels as regional leaders, we visited people who had given their lives to cross-cultural work doing projects of all kinds to bring help and Hope to faraway peoples. You rarely hear the stories of these who leave what they know, the familiar and the comfortable. How many beautiful single women have we known who in faith moved to foreign lands to learn life all over again? It's not easy or glamorous.

Ann had left her house and a fulfilling job to take the Good News to a former Soviet country.

In her first year there she had begun the strenuous task of learning language and acclimating to less than friendly surroundings. On a Tuesday evening in 1999, she put on the kettle for tea as her roommate answered a knock at the door. Suddenly a scream, and the rush of 3 masked men into the apartment shook Ann. Fierce punching battered her face as she instinctively went to see what happened. "I put my hands up swatting back, screaming, hoping to make him stop punching me. He took a gun out of his belt, pointed it in my face, and told me to shut up and stop screaming or he would kill me. Then he beat me in the head with the gun. After just a few moments I fell to the kitchen floor where he kicked me three times in the face."

The thieves were looking for money but there was none. Ann cringed in terror as they rummaged through her apartment, thinking of the prospects of what might happen next. A lucid awareness of God's presence in the midst of the bloody chaos lifted her for a moment above the present suffering and into the purpose of God, the fellowship of His suffering.

The men beat and threatened them. Their blood splattered about their apartment as Ann and her roommate fought back. Screaming and throwing things out the window, they managed to alert a neighbor. The police arrived just in time to thwart a ready butcher knife, saving their lives.

The jolting "ambulance" (jeep) ride and Soviet hospital added to the trauma. Having worked as a clinical virologist, Ann noticed the leftover blood from the last patient on the table as she walked into the x-ray room. Her face swollen, her body throbbing she called out to a doctor who was helping her with translation; earning an icy stare from the x-ray technician as someone grabbed a floor rag to wipe off the table where she would lay. They had no antibiotics, and no pain killers for her. Her pounding jaw reminded her of the kicks and punches as the Dr. stitched her head, chin and lower lip.

In the ensuing months, as she grew in understanding of the culture and in her love for the people, she found they listened a little harder when they learned she'd been beaten up by one of their people. She ministered to national women who experienced injustice and beatings as well. She had their attention in a unique way! In the criminal trial she testified on public record in a Muslim country that Jesus forgives sin!

Slow to take any credit she remarks, "You also should know I'm a wimp. I'm high maintenance. I use a blow dryer every day. In grad school I was voted most likely to bring decorative pillows and high-end cosmetics in my one bag as I went to the field. I guess I want you to know that God uses us exactly as He has created us to be." Ann is living beyond herself.

If you meet her, you'll have to strain to see a faded scar on the right side of her chin, but you won't have to strain to see the sparkle in her smile as she continues serving her God. Is that a worthy way to use a life? How quickly the end of our lives will come and we will be asking that of our own lives!

~for growth~

Ann received help and care after her horrible experience that greatly aided her recovery. While most of us won't face that level of trauma, there is often a degree of trauma in all of our lives. How can you live beyond yourself where you are now while wisely caring for your needs as well?

CHAPTER 16

BECOMING MEMBERS

"...we are members of one another."
EPHESIANS 4:25, ESV

"Unity is not an accident or something across which you stumble. It is an active choice. It is my conscious, intentional decision to move from a self-focused, entitled 'I' to becoming a member of Team – 'we'."
Global Mission Handbook, Hoke and Taylor, p.85

"Innumerable times a whole Christian community has broken down because it had sprung from a wish dream. The serious Christian, set down for the first time in a Christian community, is likely to bring with him a very definite idea of what Christian life should be and to try to realize it. But God's grace speedily shatters such dreams...By sheer grace, God will not permit us to live even for a brief period in a dream world ...The man who fashions a visionary ideal of community demands that it be realized by God, by others, and by himself. He enters the community of Christians with his demands, sets up his own law, and judges the brethren and God Himself accordingly...Christian brotherhood is not an ideal which we must realize. It is rather a reality created by God in Christ in which we may participate."

Life Together, Dietrich Bonhoeffer

It's no wonder that working together can lead to some horrendous relational shipwrecks. It's where we get down to really knowing each other and how we handle our differences. When a group works through the rigors of getting past one another's rough edges to the point of valuing differences of view and practice, it is a slight taste of heaven.

I think we all do it without realizing it... We think more highly of ourselves than we ought. It shows in our decision making, in our planning and our group dynamics.

This is a common pitfall for all of us and perhaps more particularly those of us in helping professions. We may be prone to an inflated estimate of ourselves because of our altruism or our courageous can-do philosophies. This is one of the reasons Paul reiterates the need for community, i.e. the body of believers.

"Body-life" happens in groups of believers who serve together, complementing one another's strengths, supporting, challenging and holding one another accountable. Every pioneering initiative has some faith-filled courageous 'heroes' on the front end, but they still need body-life.

When Jesus was talking with his team of twelve giving them very specific instructions regarding their work, he emphasized how important it was to wash one another's feet – that is to love one another selflessly. In fact, THAT would be how people recognized them as His disciples!

"Love one another. As I have loved you, so you must love one another. By this all men will know that you are my disciples, if you love one another."

JOHN 13:34-35, NIV

It would also validate the fact that He was sent from the Father.

"I pray also for those who will believe in me through their message, that all of them may be one, Father, just as you are in me and I am in you. May they also be in us so that the world may believe that you have sent me."

JOHN 17:21, NIV

What is it about love...? That scent of the beyond, that frees and binds, and opens up avenues and options that weren't there before? Love is powerful! No wonder God said when his people love each other they'd see something from another world!

God orchestrates unique backgrounds and experiences that prepare people for unique challenges. Paul was uniquely equipped for front-line ministry, but still needed the support and accountability of other members of the body.

"If the whole body were an eye where would the hearing be? ...now God has placed the members, each one of them in the body just as he desired..."

I CORINTHIANS 12:17, 18, NASB

Jesus worked in the context of team. Paul and Barnabas worked in the context of team. One aspect of "thinking of ourselves with sober judgment" is to welcome accountability; to view supervision as our friend and ally, as imperfect as it may be.

As ministry teams form they will inevitably cycle through the small-group stages of forming, storming, norming, performing (Bruce Tuckman) and hopefully transforming. We learn a lot about ourselves and others in the process! And if we allow conflict to carry out the purpose for which it is brought into our lives, we begin to grasp the tenets of unity.

Many of the deep lessons I've learned came from our team leading experience. There are those who consider commitment to team a distraction from their ministry. When asked to take

73

leadership responsibility, they reject it as detracting from what they really want to do. Indeed, leadership in Jesus' paradigm is about serving. But if we are unwilling to serve each other in this way, how will we ever learn to equip our brothers and sisters as servant leaders? Team is hard because our rough edges get rubbed off in close community.

When my husband and I ventured overseas in 1986, a local family met us at the airport and escorted us back to their dirt-floored abode. That was our home for the next 6 months – a fascinating and stretching experience for us. Convinced of the value of this cultural immersion we planned it for teammates who came to join us. But our perspective alone was not sufficient. As families arrived with small children the plan had to be tweaked. And it took all the voices on the team to come up with an outcome that would work for them. Seeds of conflict were avoided by hearing each other out and deciding together.

"Let us consider how to stimulate one another to love and good deeds, not forsaking our own assembling together as is the habit of some, but encouraging one another and all the more as you see the day drawing near."
HEBREWS 10:25, NASB

"He who separates himself seeks his own desire."
PROVERBS 18:1, NASB

My heart is enlarged as I work in team and see gifts that I don't have skillfully at work in others. It makes me thankful for them and promotes interdependence. It's humbling too, because there are always glitches to work through, but hearts become intertwined. I think that's his plan; it's the love he's after. Like when we see our kids enjoying one another, so God must feel when his kids do the same. Though at times I wish I had all the gifts, I soon realize the absurdity of that and am learning to relax and enjoy, value and marvel at his gifts in other people. How freeing that is!

~for growth~

How has conflict drawn you to or away from being part of a body?

What do you need to do to embrace the Body of Christ as is?

CHAPTER 17

AIRING ANCIENT

M any of the happenings in our ancient Book took place in what is now the land of Turkey. It was fascinating when we visited our colleagues there, to walk through these historic sites that tell of a different world. There, temples to gods became temples of The God... until the "prince of the power of the air" was again given leash and the temples returned to other deities. Believers are few in the land these days, so it was a distinct privilege to sit with a small group and sing "Come Lord Jesus" in Turkish!

It's as though the past is trying to get our attention when we clue in to what went on in these places. The alarming messages the apostle John wrote to the seven churches (all in present-day Turkey) are about losing our first love, being lukewarm in our faith, and bowing to other allegiances in our lives. The messages pierce from the past into our hearts today. How easy to meander into the cultures where we live, and be unaware of their influence on us. Lord, give us eyes to see and ears to hear!

When those we oversee are dealing with issues ranging from bombings to brain tumors, revolutions and ethnic cleansing, team conflicts, revoked visas and expulsions from their host country...

we cry out to Him. It costs dearly to believe and serve as aliens in unwelcoming places. One wrote:

"When experiencing unexpected times of crisis, it's easy to give in to despair. And we've definitely been feeling shock, sadness, anger, and even surprising sudden physical reactions. But thankfully with the support of our extended team and leadership, we're being reminded of truth and that nothing is impossible with God, and He can bring about redemption in and through tragedy and deep sin."

We are vividly aware of the battle between light and darkness in our host cultures... but are we aware of the unseen battle in our own lives? Are we aware that the enemy wants us to be totally unaware... or to convince us that it is old fashioned to believe there is a spiritual battle raging? All the while he works to dupe us into some form of submission to his schemes: living for the here and now, for our own riches, or pleasure or the applause of others or whatever it may be that he deceives us into believing will satisfy us.

Peter had very good intentions when he said to the Lord, "God would never let this (the crucifixion) happen to you, Lord!" Matthew 16:22, CEV. But Jesus gave him a stern wakeup call. Peter was not looking at God's interests, but at men's. How easily we do that. We make bad decisions in our hearts and need to be woken up inside.

We do sleep - our souls, that is - and drone through the days, only managing a moment of awakening here and there. Our soul drowsiness can be chronic. Sometimes I'd rather just slumber - body and soul. But then when I wake in the middle of the night for no apparent reason and can't sleep, I have to wonder. The harder, deeper struggles seem to require that extra push to deal with them. I have to decide if I'm going to engage in the wakening process... and I haven't always chosen that. But when I have, I've been amazed at the things that come up - things I didn't realize I was harboring or struggling with.

Jacob had a hard time sleeping. He was on his way home, about to face his past and his future, including his brother, Esau – who, last he knew, wanted to kill him. He chose to engage in the struggle. It was a battle over who he was and what he was trusting in... a battle between fear and believing God. He struggled with God over these things. For about twenty years he'd experienced God dealing with his deceit, anger, conniving, his bickering wives and competing sons. He'd experienced God's blessing on him despite his own shortcomings and his father-in-law's injustice. After recalling God's words to him, Jacob is at a crossroad or a "cross-river". He finally realized his unworthiness and his desperate need for God (Genesis 32:10); and God is with him in the struggle, wrestling to redefine... to re-clarify... to rename!

I want to be renamed. I need to be. I have stuff like Jacob that's stayed with me a long time. Stuff that comes up over and over. Stuff I need to leave on the other side of the river, even if it's a little bit at a time.

I think our lives are a process of renaming. Not like a change of a sticky label, but like a remaking from within. A *re-marking!* Like Colossians 3:10 puts it - "the new self...is being renewed...in the image of its Creator." (NIV)

I think Jacob would agree that it took some engaging with his Creator over a long time to get to that point.

~for growth~

Where are you in that process of being renamed?

As you sit before God silently, ask Him to reveal an identity that you are holding onto or that's holding onto you, that He wants to rename.

CHAPTER 18

BRAVING PRAYER

"For our struggle is not against flesh and blood..."
EPHESIANS 6:12, NIV

"Praying puts us at risk of getting involved in God's conditions for our lives."
Working the Angles, E. Peterson p.44

Aibek, a Muslim young man from a small village tucked in the mountains south of where we lived, was harassed at night by a demon...not the ones in our heads but an actual spiritual being that came to him to destroy him. He had heard from a foreign neighbor of another God that had power over demons. When he confided in her about his terrifying nighttime demon attacks, she said to call on the name of Jesus the next time it happened. Aibek was afraid, but also desperate. Nothing else had given him relief, so he was determined to try.

The night closed in and sleep played games with his mind. Yet the eerie presence came after him again. Heavy on his chest it came, choking him. In a smothered gasp he cried out the Name of Jesus and immediately felt the demon push off his chest...as though terrified of that Name.

Never had he been able to get rid of it before! Even his religious leaders had no answer. What was this power? Who is this God? The next day he rushed to tell his neighbor what had happened. She told him more about this powerful One who could free him. Utterly grateful, Aibek gave his life over to the Strong God that day.

His family was shamed that he would denounce their tradition and follow a foreign way. They had to save face; they had to punish him for their honor. The beatings couldn't make him recant his new faith. But he feared for his life so he fled to the city; he had to start a new life. When some fellow believers took him in, he found a job, and the way opened before him in the midst of his struggles. The years passed. Many were struggling to make a living in those early post-Soviet days, and Aibek eventually became the most economically stable member of his whole family. Those who were threatening him before were now seeking him out for help.

It all started with a prayer; a single desperate cry to God.

How do we lose this sense of need for prayer?

Like in John Mayer's song, "Stop This Train," we occasionally want to ask time for a little mercy. It's going by so fast and we can't catch up. Time knows no mercy of course, but we can choose to pause, in order to get more out of whatever just happened... and to meet the next hours with better perspective. I see it as taking a moment to rebel against the fastness of life.

We all want to stop at times and relish the moments, or process what just happened, and prayer is a chance to do this! But do we take the time to really pray?

We must go with care, not glibly. It's a chance to unload... to pour out our hearts honestly... and then to hear from the One who knows us. Are we willing for that? To hear and respond? Or are we afraid of it, holding a distorted view of what might happen if we listened to God and his Word and responded with all of our hearts?

I know it saddens God when we don't involve him in our lives. Often, he talks about how he longed to do something for his children but that they were unwilling. They thought they knew better. What a slam against our Creator who knows so well what we need and want. Listen to the pain in his voice as he travails over his kids.

> "'Ah, stubborn children,' declares the Lord, 'who carry out a plan, but not mine, and who make an alliance but not of my Spirit...without asking for my direction."
>
> ISAIAH 30:1,2, ESV

> "My dear son...my darling child...my heart yearns for him".
>
> JEREMIAH 31:20, NASB

> "O Jerusalem...how I longed to gather you...but you were unwilling."
>
> MATT. 23:37, NIV

> "If only you had paid attention to my commands, your peace would have been like a river,
>   your righteousness like the waves of the sea."
>
> ISAIAH 48:18, NIV

We forget how intimately He knows us, how detailed His understanding is of how we're made, of our circumstances, our pasts, and even of our thoughts right now. We think we know better, and we want what we want. Maybe we feel danger in really engaging with the One Who Knows Better, since we might have to change our minds.

But prayer helps us transcend this life to get new perspective. It's where the very common enters the throne room of God;

a place where worship gives us eyes to see the greater Reality. And it also includes fight. Because we have an enemy that is set against us. So there will be resistance when we choose to go the higher way. We have to expect it or we'll be thrown off kilter when we pray.

"The story of our life is the story of a long and brutal assault on your heart by the one who knows what you could be and fears it." Waking the Dead, John Eldredge, p. 37

~for growth~

When's the last time you really poured your heart out to God? Find a time; put it on your calendar!

Choose one obstacle to prayer that you will face with faith and drive the enemy crazy with your belief.

CHAPTER 19

REASONING WITH GOD

Comparison, competition, coveting, complacency

It's quite natural to be fixed on these four actions and not even realize how much thinking, energy and effort goes into them. I am a competitive person. I competed on a gymnastic team in my junior high years and gained great discipline in "buffeting my body and making it my slave" 1 Corinthians 9:27, NAS. It served me well, though in this fallen world competitiveness tends to take us down wrong paths. The desire for excellence in the spiritual realm is a good thing. But in our fallenness we resort to comparing ourselves with others we deem spiritual and conclude that their way is the definition of spirituality or the way to become better at life. We inadvertently compete and work toward a goal that wasn't meant for us, all the time coveting the honor or feeling of accomplishment... or arrival to a state of goodness that is revered. Or we give up, thinking we've made enough sacrifices, we've pushed hard enough, and it's time to take a break from growth.

After some years overseas, I reached a point where I was comfortable in the foreign language, and felt somewhat accomplished in living and working in a context of faraway sacrifice. With that

I started to slack a bit... slack at realizing how far I still had to go, how much I still desperately needed God and others. Then, wouldn't you know it, I'd meet someone who was far better than me in doing all that I was doing, at least as I saw it. And I had to stop and listen to my thoughts. What was I saying to myself?

"I wish I could speak as freely and clearly as she does in this language." (comparison)
"I need to study harder and work more at this." (competition)
"She is so loved by the local people. I want that!" (coveting)
"I'll never get to that level." (complacency)

There was truth in all those statements, but I often came to the wrong conclusion without letting the Lord speak into my thoughts. He has a lot to say about these things if we'll listen.

Wishing to speak freely and clearly in another language (or my own for that matter!) is a good thing. But do I wish it so I can be better than her or so I can fulfill what I've been asked to do? My "race" is different from hers, my gifts and responsibilities are other. Can I take the good from that thought - the motivation to speak clearly - and ask that it be purified for the unique purpose He's assigned to me?

Hard work and study are good. Unless the only reason I'm doing it is to outshine another. Can I take that push from another's success and turn it into motivation to seek excellence for the sake of those in my world who need care and encouragement? Of course, when we recognize our wrong motives, the enemy may tempt us to abandon the reach for success altogether. But not God. He would have us lean into our growth, wary of the tendency to pride and competition, yet holding onto Him to transform us.

Wanting to be loved by others is another good thing that, like desiring success, can be susceptible to corruption. Do I want it at another's expense? At the expense of my own First Love? To lift up my faltering ego? Or do I want it so others will be attracted to a higher way of life crafted by their Creator? Can I confess my bent toward self-centeredness, and choose freedom to want others to love me, and freedom to let them not as well? Can I be ok with either?

Getting to a certain level of objectivity in examining our thoughts is a worthy goal! We should expect to find sin there. But if we are willing to take it to the Lover of our souls where there is no condemnation, we can join him in his work within us. I think he loves that. Though we are hard bent toward sin, God's people throughout the ages have heard His invitation:

"Come let us reason together..."

ISAIAH 1:18, ESV

~for growth~

Which of the 4 C words do you struggle with the most?

(Comparison, competition, coveting, complacency)

What does that tell you about yourself?

CHAPTER 20

LEADING SELF

*"Teach us to number our days, that we may present to
You a heart of wisdom."*

PSALM 90:12, NASB

This morning I went to make some coffee. Seeing there was only a little bit, I got out the grinder to grind more coffee and saw the shelf where the grinder was sitting was quite dirty. So I ground some beans thinking, I've got to clean that shelf. When I finished grinding I cleaned the shelf with a rag and cleaner... at which time I remembered we wanted to fill that same spray bottle with vinegar to get rid of a bad smell under our sink. So, I emptied the spray bottle and filled it with vinegar to stalk the offensive odor. I sprayed deeply into the crevices... while noticing the garbage needed to be taken out... when my husband, working in the next room asked if the coffee was done. I realized I hadn't turned on the coffee!

Focus.

How do we keep our focus? How do we even know what it should be?

What you want the rest of your life to look like is a serious consideration. Not everyone regains the same degree of strength or mobility after a major surgery. When my friend had completed the first third of her physical therapy following a knee replacement, her therapist congratulated her for finishing the most painful part. But he warned that the next two-thirds would be mentally harder. "Honestly, this is where a lot of people say, 'enough', but here's the key: The work you do in these next two-thirds will determine the quality of your life moving forward. You can simply start walking around to the extent that you want to walk the rest of your life or you can build up strength for a totally different rest of your life."

Are you up for a totally different rest of your spiritual life?

Jotham was! (2 Chronicles 27:6) He was the Son of King Uzziah who was a descendant of Caleb, one of the twelve who spied out the promised land, and one of only two who had the courage and faith to obey God and go in.

Uzziah, Jotham's father, one of the kings of Judah around 650 B.C. reigned fifty-two years. Fifty-two! It was the longest of any of Judah's kings (besides Manasseh whose reign was "bad"). Uzziah did much good. He walked with God, did humanitarian projects, furthered the kingdom, rebuilt and fortified walls, broke down and destroyed other walls, had a well-trained army for which he provided weapons and war "machines designed by skillful men". He had fame and honor. Then toward the end of his life there was something going on in his heart that was unchecked, misdirected... and I imagine it wasn't an overnight descent. I'd venture to say it was very subtle and had been growing within him for years.

There's a hint toward this in 2 Chronicles 26:19. Uzziah knew he was overstepping his bounds going into a holy place that only consecrated priests were supposed to enter. They were trying to warn him and help him see, but what did he do? He raged...

RAGED. Where did that come from?! The conditions for "instant rage" don't grow overnight. Note that it doesn't say he argued, disagreed, got upset... and then raged. He felt somehow, that he was above this law. How did he get from "He was greatly helped" to raging at the priests? (2 Chronicles 26:15, 19 NIV)

He was rushed out of the inner sanctuary because leprosy broke out on his forehead. He wouldn't listen to anyone else so God stepped in. He was promptly demoted, lived the rest of his days in isolation, and died in shame. (It was the year he died that Isaiah saw the Lord in Isaiah 6.)

While he was still living, his son Jotham took over. Imagine how it impacted him, having seen what happened, maybe having suspected that his Dad's spiritual life was dulling. There may have been other incidents of raging... evidence of attitudes that differed from the younger, God-seeking Dad he'd known. Seeing the severity of God's judgment on one of the greatest kings of Judah probably put the fear of God in Jotham. He and Isaiah both saw first-hand what happened to someone who had been very faithful, and then failed to finish strong.

Jotham continued some of the good work. (2 Chronicles 27:1-6)

- Rebuilt the upper gate of the temple
- Did extensive work on the wall at the hill of Ophel
- Built towns, forts, towers
- Built fortresses (because of these Jerusalem was protected later when Jotham's grandson Hezekiah reigned); he was forward-looking enough to see the need to guard from attack.
- Made war on God's enemies and conquered
- And "ordered his ways". 2 Chronicles 27:6 ESV (I think this refers to how he did all of the above.)

Other translations describe this as "prepared his ways", was "careful to live in obedience", "walked steadfastly", or (my favorite) "directed" his ways. What is the obvious thrust of these colorful descriptors?

He consciously decided and acted on it. The Hebrew word used is also found in Jeremiah 30:20 with the meaning of "establish, set up or direct". He directed himself, like Daniel when he "made up his mind" or like Paul said to Timothy "watch yourself with all diligence". In other words, "be aware of yourself so you can re-direct where needed". We need constant re-direction or realignment and maybe more so in our latter days. This passage screams to us. Do we hear it?

Self-leadership, as some call it, will determine our leadership of others. Our leadership of others flows out of our leadership of ourselves!

Something that helps me do this is lists. Some people hate them, some people love them, but somehow we all need them. Lists come in all forms now: paper, electronic, audio, white board, post-it notes. Part of ordering our days has to do with lists. Like listing our priorities and determining our focus for the hour, day, week or month. A lot of our lives depend on how we get ourselves organized and focused. Having had to move many times during my adult life, I've learned the value of clarifying my priorities and ordering my days accordingly.

There was a time in my life when I made lists of goals that I had for our kids: things to work on and pray for in their character, academic goals when I was homeschooling. Learning personal and professional growth planning as part of my graduate studies helped greatly with these things. We just need so much help to focus. We are people easily distracted...with good things. We need to learn to distinguish the good from the best. Paul said it this way in Philippians 1:9,10, ESV: "It is my prayer that your love may abound...with knowledge and all discernment, so that you may approve what is excellent." (or "discern what is best" NIV).

What we do with our time, how we number our ordinary days: tells us a lot about ourselves.

"The temptation to compromise basic Christian values – love, community, truth telling, confession and reconcil-iation, silent listening and waiting on God for discernment – for the sake of expedience is very great."
<u>Strengthening the Soul of Your leadership</u>,
Ruth Barton, p. 27.

As we grow older we are more tempted to be careless in ordering our ways before the Lord. As leaders, we are still mostly followers!

"Growth cannot happen without the powerful respect for the reality of indwelling evil and its insidious work through self-deceit. It leads us to lie to God, ourselves and one another." "Investing your life Wisely,"
Gordon MacDonald

Self-leadership is a huge part of leading others. It stems from self-awareness, i.e. knowing ourselves (our strengths, flaws, ten-dencies) and understanding how we affect others.

~for growth~

What might King Uzziah have neglected as he progressed in years?

What rebukes from others or from God might have been brushed aside? (Proverbs 1:23)

In your personal life and leadership how can you order your ways?

What is one thing that is coming to mind that should change?

"Ponder the path of your feet." Proverbs 4:26, ESV

CHAPTER 21

WHIRLING WHIRLED VIEWS

"The theory to which we ascribe will determine what we see."

Albert Einstein

Does it really matter what we believe about the origin of life? It can be quite convenient to believe there is no God. Just as it can be quite convenient to believe there is one.

"There are only two possible explanations as to how life arose: spontaneous generation or a supernatural creative act of God. There is no other possibility. Spontaneous generation was scientifically disproved one hundred and twenty years ago by Louis Pasteur and others but that just leaves us with one other possibility, that life came as a supernatural act of creation by God. But if I cannot accept that philosophically because I do not want to believe in God, I choose to believe in that which I know is scientifically impossible."

Dr. George Ward, Professor Emeritus at Harvard, Nobel Prize Winner in Biology in 1971

I feel sorry for atheists. I'm no scientist but in Anatomy and Physiology class I was rather convinced that this incredible machine we wear as our outer shell has a Designer beyond our imagination. But for an atheist that body is all there is. No inner anything. It takes faith to believe all that complex design came from nothing with no purpose, no reason, no hope, no love; just chance. So, their bottom line really takes more faith than ours.

It is actually easier to believe that there's Something behind it all - that brought the visible into being. Twentieth century science brought to light the complexity of the "simple cell" which Darwin himself predicted would refute his theory. This theory of "irreducible complexity" (Total Truth, Nancy Pearcy, p.187) shows how a cell needs to have all its components in mature form for it to work as it does. So, the simple cell defies evolution.

Then there's DNA, with specified, customized information that goes well beyond the material enzymes and chromosomes...

So you have to consider, right?! If there really is a Designer who has given us information about what really is, then we need to sit up and pay attention. Because whatever he says should work - for all of the universe, and for me.

But if there is NOT a designer - no purpose, no prescribed meaning or reason - then one person's thinking is as good as another's. Who has the right to say otherwise? If the state dictates what's best for society (including for you), who's to say they have no right? If Stalin mandates brutal population relocations with no care for human suffering, who's to criticize? If there's no purpose and we're all headed to nowhere anyway - to each, his own!

Joseph Stalin's daughter said of her father's death, "It was as if he were shaking his fist at God in one final act of defiance." (https://thecenterbham.org/2015/03/23/what-would-it-mean-if-he-really-did-rise/) Evidently Stalin's will for there not to be a God could not make it come true. He couldn't will God out of existence, just because God wasn't who he wanted him to be.

The fallacy in the atheist's thinking is that it is "based on fact". It's not. The fact is, no one was there to prove the "big bang". It is just a theory, contrary to popular belief! The scientific method insists "theory - until empirically proven".

Credible evidence of microevolution in no way conflicts with evidence of intelligent design. The evidence is overwhelming that the Creator God is who he said he is. In fact, there's more evidence that Jesus Christ rose from the dead than that Julius Caesar ever lived. And do we question Ceasar's life? Any honest historian acknowledges that the manuscript evidence for the Old and New Testaments is far beyond that of any other manuscripts of their day.

When our family moved into the aftermath of the Soviet Union, we saw the loss of dignity, the meaninglessness, the lack of life in life. That's what "no God" leads to. It strips humanity of spirit and soul; of initiative, morality and meaning. The Soviets we encountered had good reason to believe as they did, but when they looked at the love and hope in our lives, they wondered. And some found their souls.

Our daughter enjoys conversations with people who say they're atheists because she cares about them and is genuinely interested in what brought them to their beliefs. She was working in an ice cream shop and got to know another worker who started darting her with questions. Rachel spoke of her convictions about certain things explaining what and why she believed. Her new friend said, "I want convictions!" ☺

There is "eternity in our hearts". (Ecclesiastes 3:11) "We were made for another world. Our lives are meant for so much more." (Switchfoot, Meant to Live). Humankind just can't seem to get away from this one.

But then there's doubt. Doubt comes unbidden and unwelcome, like that mafia man at the door in our cold little office in Central Asia. At times our crazy hearts condemn us, and though we know truth and have been thoroughly convinced, doubt knocks at the door. And though we don't offer it a seat, tea or even entrance, it stands around to taunt and whisper. When fear goes out, doubt can come in. I shake my head in unbelief at how persistent it can be, and I even smile and say to it, "Are you still trying to win?" I've seen too much and felt and watched and heard. History, fulfillment of prophecy, archeology, joy and meaning in life defy doubt. Yet it lurks. So we have to be vigilant. There's no promise for those who doubt; and lots of promises for those who believe! I choose to stand on the side of belief and with God's help I win! Our hearts may condemn us but "God is greater than our hearts." 1 John 3:20, NIV

~for growth~

When doubts come, what is your bottom line?

How do you navigate the whirled views of our world?

How do you fight the enemy of your soul who weasels into your mind with half-truths and false promises?

Are you aware of his schemes?

CHAPTER 22

ASKING BIG

Going after Grit – From our four kids

"You have not because you ask not..."
JAMES 4:2, KJB

As I was in labor with our first child, after about 30 hours the Dr. said to my husband, "The baby's not moving down fast enough; after the next contraction we'll take her in for a C-section." My heart dropped. We were in a foreign country having our first baby in our home. I didn't know enough about the medical system in this place, only that Dan wouldn't be allowed in the room with me if I delivered at the hospital. We were a bit naive. Exhausted, I cried within, ready to let it be. I leaned back on my husband as he prayed out loud. The next contraction came and perhaps with the prayer I had relaxed enough to let the baby come out, because right then he did! What a relief and joy to see our sweet baby boy. We named him Luke and were entranced with him.

He has a way of grabbing your heart. Maybe part of it was because he was the first of the grandchildren on my side of the family. We all fell in love with him. He practically came out speaking full sentences and kept us busy. ☺ He grabbed life full force and wanted to do everything himself. When facing disappointment of not having things other kids had, I remember him at around seven years old saying, "This song is like me mom!" referring to a kids' song about not having all the toys but the richness of having the Lord.

Music seemed to articulate his soul. I'll never forget when the song "Who am I?" by Casting Crowns came out. He was driving and pulled the car over saying, "Mom, listen to this song!" We sat there and listened to the amazing words. It was such a sweet moment together. I realized God was helping him (and me!) grasp these deep truths that carried him through so many transitions.

As a junior high student, he wrestled with the fact that he couldn't be on a football team because of where we lived. I told him of my choice to give up a sport I loved when I was new in my faith. His words hit hard. He said, "Well at least you had a choice." Wow. What could I say but to turn him to the Lord.

His high school guidance counselor said of him, "He's his own best advocate". He went after relationships and opportunities. Though he'd grown up overseas he had an abiding love for American football. He would gather kids on Saturdays in the former Soviet Union to play football!

He had a desire. He loved God. And though we can demand nothing of God, we can ask. He is a perfect, caring Father who loves to give good gifts to his kids. So, we laid it out before God, who led him to a high school where a former college football coach began teaching him the basics. He picked up bits here and there and learned from anyone who knew the game. When he returned to the USA for his junior year in high school, he contacted the coach and ended up making the team! Though he didn't get to play much, he loved it and was the team's best fan. And he kept working – speed training, practice, studying the game. What he lacked in size he made up for in hard work. He thought big, and played big,.... and he was fast.

Meanwhile he was applying for the Naval Academy. Our kids, having grown up outside of the US became quite patriotic. They saw what other people lived with and without. They saw how governments can wreck a people and their dignity. And they appreciate the cost of freedom.

After the grueling application process, he received a nomination from congressman Charlie Dent and was accepted.

The ones who make it that far get a fancy certificate congratulating them just for being accepted. We dropped him off with tears and trembling on Initiation Day. Here's what he wrote about what he found there:

"It was called Farragut field, a turf field tucked in a back corner of the Naval Academy grounds, surrounded by the bay along two sides. This was home to a small group of brothers. They were often regarded as the hardest working athletes on the Yard (that was our word for campus, stemming from Naval yard, or ship yard). In our minds there was no question, and our coaches seemed to be determined to prove that every day anew. Only those who have experienced August humidity in Annapolis can begin to appreciate what it might be like to play for a light weight football team; a sport that combines every aspect of American football with the idea that there can be a size restriction, i.e. cutting weight (think wrestling or boxing weight classes). It was not uncommon for guys to practice in full sweats under their pads in an attempt to lose weight. It was called Sprint Football - we prided ourselves on our speed but even more so, our endurance. Every

season began with the understanding that the next three months (seasons were short due to the size of the league – seven teams) would be the most grueling of the year. With that however, came the absolute certainty that we would be the toughest and most prepared team to step on the field come game day.

It started during what is known as Plebe summer; seven weeks of military indoctrination, a summer of humiliation. No one enjoys it but everyone goes through it. There was however one aspect of the summer that made the rest bearable. It was called sports-period; a three-hour block of late afternoon when we escaped the demands and outrages of our upper-class cadre to participate in a sport of our choosing. Most varsity level teams used this time to begin evaluating incoming freshmen for acceptance onto the team come fall. After being woken at 0545 to spend an hour and a half PT-ing (physical training) followed by being run all over campus for the next six hours – no one showed up to sports-period ready to give 100%. Knowing that, the coaches asked for nothing less. The approach was: no one made this team based on physical talent alone, your heart and mental fortitude were far more important. And so, it began: July 2006, Annapolis, temperature: high 90's, humidity: 100%, felt like: 110%.

I had heard bits and pieces about the Sprint program but did not know much about it. I attended the informational meeting and decided I had nothing to lose. I would try out. I had never even dreamed of playing past high school, and here I was at one of seven schools in the nation (world for that matter) that offered anything like it. I had only played two years of football in my entire life. In summary, I had no idea what I was doing. The rest of these guys had been playing for the better part of a decade, some even attending prep-schools for an extra year of development before going to college. It started as a complete blur. On top of the hundreds of things I was being demanded to learn from a military perspective, I now had football drills, schemes and concepts to memorize. My legs were jello and my mind was mush, but I soon realized that if I had ever wanted something in my life, it was to make this team.

Throughout those summer weeks we sweat and bled into that Farragut turf, building a bond that extends far beyond football. In the years since it has been referred to as a brotherhood more often than a team, and that is exactly what I was fighting to be a part of. Through God's blessing, amazingly, I did become a part, and after four painful years at the Academy I can say God got me through that school using that team. It was the one thing I truly enjoyed during my time there. My childhood dream had actually become a reality!"

Luke Scott

Our desires and requests may seem far-fetched. And we get plenty of 'no' answers. But often I think we have not because we ask not. God answers. Search your heart...then ask!

~for growth~

What is in your heart that you've hesitated to ask God for?

Can you zero in on what you really want?

CHAPTER 23

TRUSTING FOR MORE

"I will counsel you with my loving eye on you"
-GOD, PSALM 32:8, NIV

O ur second son Brad started out, as nature has
it, in the shadow of his older
brother. He was quieter and
quite the observer; more cau-
tious and less sure of himself
yet very astute, taking in
everything around him. He
became quite the entertainer giving dramatic presentations of
things he noticed. In his early teens having already experienced
several major moves to different cultures in his young life, he
came to a crossroads:

"After my freshman year of high school, I was tired of making
new friends, angry about moving a lot, introverted, and insecure
with myself. I didn't want to reach out or try to make friends again.
I was living lonely, just with family all the time. I was in public
school in America for the first time, played sports and connected

with people superficially. I didn't go any deeper probably due to the barrier of knowing I was leaving again.

At youth group I had some friends but no desire to go deep since I felt no one knew me. I didn't know what I wanted, and had a lot of insecurity. I worried about what people thought about me. It was a heavy burden. I didn't want to care how others thought of me, but in everything I was so consumed with whether they approved of me. Since I didn't have an idea of what I wanted or who I was, I lived for the approval of people.

I was trying to decide where I was going to go to school. My parents were going back to Central Asia and I could go to an International school in Thailand or stay with them. Going back to Central Asia was my comfort zone. I had a few friends, a very small school, and it's what I wanted to do. They were my only friends. I didn't feel judged for being different. I really feared going anywhere else. During the year at public school it was so hard to break into any circles. There were a lot of superficial friends but I knew I was an outsider to them.

So, as I was trying to make my decision, my Dad took me out to breakfast to talk about it. He encouraged me to think about going to the international school. It would open up opportunities even though I would be away from him and mom. I would only have a few classmates in the small school where they lived, giving me limited challenge and opportunity. But I had fear about breaking into new friend groups and a new school. I hated that. I wanted to just be in one place like everybody else (or so I thought). I ate a ton of food at that breakfast, then I ate a massive blueberry muffin. ☺

Somehow, I think God used that to speak to me. When my Dad let me get the muffin this showed me that he was not going to run my life and that he would let me choose what I wanted.

Then a few weeks before we left, I was at youth group. I remember thinking I hated who I was and told God I didn't want to stay that way. I started praying even before the worship time, which went for a while and I ended up praying for a long time and never stood up. Somehow, I saw the big picture perspective that if I stayed the way I was, I was not going to be effective or do anything significant or ever love people. I saw that and cried out to God. I choose to cry out to him and knew I couldn't change on my own and decided to ask Him for change that night. He spoke to me and I had a confidence in Him that I was going to be able to be different; that I could get rid of the fear of another transition coming. This was a lot of talking to God back and forth between my deciding I will change and acknowledging I needed God's help to change. I wasn't going to change who I was overnight just because I decided to.

But then I had peace. I decided to go to Thailand. On the plane over I was reading and writing in my journal. I prayed the same thing. Lord, I'm going to start with a clean slate. God had given an opportunity to shut down and re-set who I was; to choose him as God, and put my security and identity in him. This was the biggest transitional moment in my life. I couldn't have changed like this if I had stayed in the same place geographically, so this was a perfect chance to move ahead and make a change. I saw it as a gift.

Even though we want to change, if we stay geographically in the same place it's much harder. Amazingly he took the fear away, fear that rooted back to me putting my identity in what others thought of me. I stopped worrying and fearing people. In the new place, I was free to become what I wanted and he wanted me to be.

A second step in the process of deciding to change was following through and confirming to myself, yes, I'm going to do this. My sister Rachel starting new at this school too, couldn't believe what she saw. She felt like she had a whole different brother. She woke up to a night and day difference. I was instantly able to reach out and make friends and began to really seek God for myself in a way that I never cared to before this.

I remember she said that she never thought I would teach her to love people because she thought I never cared about anyone. It was a drastic jumpstart. I was free to love others no matter if I was different or if they didn't like me. There was freedom from being timid or shy. I wanted to be able to do what I thought was right no matter what others thought. People wouldn't believe me when I said I was an introvert. I started really enjoying others." Brad Scott

Dan and I noticed and were amazed at God's work, his answers to prayer as we continued to walk with our kids through this crazy life of transitions.

Photo – Ethan Froelich

~for growth~

What are your reactions to transitions in your life?

Can you find someone to help you work through them?

How can you take advantage of them for new starts?

CHAPTER 24

Embracing Life As Is
("life should be easy" and other lies)

"Life is difficult. Once we truly know that life is difficult –
once we truly understand and accept it – then life is no
longer difficult."

Peck, M. Scott. Road Less Traveled,
New York: Touchstone, 1988

Late October 2009 I got a call that no mom wants to get. Her usual cheerful voice was shaken and struggling, and my heart sank. Our daughter, Rachel was in a hospital with a broken foot in Greece where she was doing her freshman year of college. We were in Thailand a quarter of the globe away with no resources to get to her. I broke down... She had overcome bitterness toward God in her high school years; now this, in her first semester away from us. Why now, when we weren't there for her?

I wanted to go. I was mad at her for not being more careful, mad that I couldn't be there to help, mad that God (though I knew better) didn't "protect" her. Wait, didn't he say something about hitting your foot on a rock?!

> "For he will command his angels concerning you to guard you in all your ways; they will lift you up in their hands, so that you will not strike your foot against a stone."
>
> PS 91:11, 12, NIV

So where were the angels that day? Taking a break? I had another one of those talks with the Lord.

But I had a sense that her spiritual feet were the things he was concerned with and that this was a journey he was taking her on. It didn't make me feel much better at the moment. I knew his hand was on her and her heart was his. But I hated that this was happening in her first year away from us; and when she had so much travel and adventure planned. But God was greatly protecting her in more ways than we realized. There's much more to protection than just the physical realm.

Her love for rock climbing took her to some risky, but gorgeous spots. She and two friends were out exploring on the cliffs above Athens, overlooking the Aegean Sea. It was a perfect climbing day. She was mesmerized with the luring beauty of Greece. A bit over-confident, she led the route, meaning her anchor points were always below her on the cliff since she clipped the rope in as she climbed. Eager to get a view from the top, she got her gear in order, tied the figure eight follow-through, checked her harness and examined the cliff. Finding some good holds, she set out making the way for the others. She clipped in at four meters, then at eight meters....as she stretched to clip the next one, the pinch grip of her left hand and a small right toe chip were her only holds. Shakily, she clipped the quick draw into the bolt. Trying to breathe and ignore the fact that she was fifteen feet above her last clip, she lifted the rope to clip into the quick draw, her foot slipped and she tumbled down the rugged face, feeling the jerk of the rope as she hit her foot hard on an overhang jutting out of the cliff.

Here's how she described it:

"Never Skip Greek Class"

Rock climbing or Greek class? These were my options one sunny Tuesday afternoon in October 2009. Rock climbing won out, big surprise. Somehow the call of the cliffs on the mountains towering above Athens was a little stronger than the prospects of two hours shut inside a classroom with only the small window next to me reminding me of all the things I was missing outside. If ever there was a transformative experience, that day was it, if not of my own personality, then definitely of my life.

One lost grip, one eighteen-foot fall, one broken ankle and my life went from days of soccer, volleyball, basketball, and weekends on the crew of a sailboat in the Aegean Sea, to absolutely stationary months with an elevated, casted, and throbbing ankle. What did I learn? Well, at least one thing – never skip Greek Class.

A broken ankle sounds trivial stated so tersely on paper, but trivialities can be life changing! I'd been in Greece for less than three weeks when my ankle swelled to three times its usual size in response to an unwelcome collision with a rock jutting out of the cliff I was doing my best to climb. We had off-roaded in a jeep and then hiked to get to the base of the cliff, so to get back, I half hobbled, half rode on my friend Johnny's back down the mountain. Then, I clenched my teeth and tried to cradle my leg as the jeep bounced down the mountain. I fixated on the cloud in the sky that looked like God's forearm stretched out against the red sunset. I was convinced it was just a bad sprain, I'd heard those could be even more painful than breaks and was happy to believe it.

Sitting in the waiting room, anxiously protecting my foot from careless wheel-chair-pushers and turning my eyes away from open wounds, I wondered how many hours it would be until the number over the emergency room door would match the one on my ticket. I felt like I was in a less efficient version of the deli line at the grocery store, and a couple hours later was beginning to think socialized health care isn't such a good idea. At this point I still knew no Greek (skipping class probably didn't help) and only one person was allowed in with me, so our one Greek speaker – a guy I'd met less than a week before– was the only one with me in the overcrowded, emergency room in downtown Athens.

If it was broken, I thought it would just be a crack, so when I didn't see any hairlines on the x-ray I thought this was good news. But the doctor quickly assured me in his broken English that the two bones I was looking at used to be one, and this was the worst break I could have had. I was almost amused, despite the news, at the harshness of his announcement, with no attempt at breaking it to me kindly, a clear reminder I was no longer in the tell-me-what-I-want-to-hear country of America. My parents were across the globe in Thailand, my brothers on the other side of the world in the US, and I was sitting on the bed of an emergency room in Greece shocked and alone, trying not to cry.

How can I describe how much being active and playing sports means to me? My greatest joy is being with my team on a court or field. Sports helps me process and rejoice and let down and work hard and be intense and lead and be part of something bigger and be me. I couldn't imagine a life without it.

I tried to be strong on the phone with my parents when I finally got in touch with them a couple days later. I knew it was probably harder on my mom than me, feeling like she couldn't be there for me. But God was there, in tiny and huge ways that felt like hugs. My grandfatherly Bible College Director had me immediately transferred to a private clinic. His childhood friend with deep Athenian roots was with him when they first visited. With only three fingers left on his hand and numerous scars from motorcycle accidents, he was all too familiar with the Greek medical system. He liked me because I was tough and because I had a motorcycle back in Thailand too.

After making a few phone calls and pulling a few strings, he arranged for the three top doctors in Athens, each from a different hospital, to come to the clinic and perform my surgery! I could write a whole series of memoirs on the ways God took care of me, from my roommate at the hospital being a nurse who worked there, to the school campus being small enough for me to get around on crutches, to the close community that was more than willing to help, to a perfectly timed Christmas break in Thailand that allowed me to swim and rehab in ways I couldn't have in Greece. Calling to me, the inside cover of my Bible was filled with the "All verses" during my hospital stay. My dad gave them to me, a challenge to praise "in all things, for all things, and at all times." I now had a mission statement for the months ahead.

It hurt to watch my soccer team play without me, and to watch the sails of the Morning Star hoisted without my help, but I could still dig into the Word and develop deep friendships and richly enjoy my year in Greece.

The real test of faith and heart was the year after the original accident. After a year out of sports, I was finally getting back into it at the beginning of the year at Wheaton College. I was overjoyed to be running, jumping, cutting, playing Frisbee, basketball, volleyball, this whole trial and injury was behind me.

Then things started going downhill, seemingly without reason. It started with a little pain in my foot, I thought this was just a minor glitch. But it kept hurting. I stopped playing sports completely. The pain kept increasing. I started riding my bike everywhere, walking as little as possible. The pain kept increasing. Before I knew it, I was back on crutches, seeking second, third and fourth opinions because every doctor kept telling me this condition was going to be for the rest of my life. I broke the worst bone possible, and many people with this break never walk again. I was told things would never go back to normal; that chronic pain would keep getting worse my whole life, with more surgeries almost certainly ahead.

I thought the hardest part was over, actually I'd thought the whole thing was over. The months of crutching in Greece seemed like a cake-walk compared to the ambiguous, no-end-in-sight tread this was becoming. With an end in view, I was able to cling to God and keep my joy and choose praise and even to influence different people throughout the process. I didn't do nearly as well the second time around. And writing this I can't help but think how hard other people's lives are – lost parents or close friends, abuse or deep wounds by others. I acknowledge how incredibly blessed I am and realize in the large scheme of things, this really isn't that big a deal.

That being said, it still struck at my heart. Correction: it's still striking at my heart, so even though on the whole it's a little deal, it still feels like a big one. I just don't know why God would make me to love something so much if He was going to take it away, not just for a short lesson, but forever.

So, I'm nowhere near done with this, and I'm nowhere near "learning the lesson" I'm supposed to – I don't even know what it is. But it has made me depend on God. It has MADE me depend on Him. I really couldn't do it without Him. I almost didn't write that line because its cliché sound grates, but it's true. The pain every second step reminds me how weak I am, how much I need God. As the temperature in the Illinois winter decreases, the pain increases, and the more often "Your grace is sufficient for me" runs through my mind.

There are days of hope too. Times when I walk without pain, and even days when my ankle lets me get away with running for a bit without increasing the pain so much that I can't walk the next day. Whatever the doctors say, God can heal me if He wants to. I guess more than anything, I want to lean into whatever lesson He has. I want to respond in a way that glorifies Him, even if I don't have any definite conclusions. And tomorrow if I had to choose between class and rock climbing, I'd still choose rock climbing. I guess I haven't learned my lesson. Rachel Scott Wood

~for growth~

Can we honestly bring those annoying life trials, big and small, to the Orchestrator of our lives?

CHAPTER 25

CALLING IT OUT AS A GAME

"When passion fades, discipline holds."
Cheryl Beckett, martyr

On a slow day during the late February dry season in Thailand, my friend's voice sputtered on the other end of the phone. Panicking she could hardly get the words out. Her daughter and our son had just been in a motorcycle accident and were heading to the emergency room. Kelvin, our son was in shock, his friend was sobbing as they lay on the stretchers. Holding back our fears we tried to comfort them as we waited. I knew God was up to something.

Kelvin was in ninth grade and it was half-way through the basketball season. Chosen to be on varsity team as a freshman, he was stoked, but had just found out he wouldn't be playing in a tournament due to a grade discrepancy. He was reeling over this and mad at the world, because basketball was what he lived for. He says:

"The whole year I had put everything into basketball even though it hadn't been a good year for me. I felt I was always down in other areas of life and wasn't performing well. So now it felt like

117

a downward spiral toward wrong motives, wrong focus, wrong identity. How I felt about myself sprang from my performance at basketball and because it wasn't going well, I was not feeling good about myself.

Then on Feb 27, 2007 we had a half-day of school, so I was going to the pool with some friends. I rode on the back of a motor-cycle and as we slowed to make a turn a truck barreled toward us hitting us broad side. My head (in a helmet) hit the wind-shield and cracked it, and something pounded into my leg. I was thrown from the bike and in shock. I didn't know what happened. From my stupor I tried to get up then saw the blood and felt the strangeness in my leg. After days in hospital, x-rays, surgery, a cast, and crutches... frustration set in, not being able to play or do anything. I was pretty chill about it which was kind of weird. It didn't hit me as hard as maybe it should have. Somehow, I didn't cry or outwardly didn't blame my friend but I definitely treated her differently. In a way subconsciously I thought, "You owe me now, I don't owe you anything". Later in our senior year I told her face to face not to ever think of that as her fault. She needed to hear that from me and accept it. The truck driver was at fault and ended up paying for everything.

I had a false hope of returning to life quicker. One visit to the doctor was very discouraging because my leg wasn't healing right. I broke two casts trying to walk and play. I had to get a new cast that would set the bone in the right direction. More waiting...

I never considered not getting back to level and did everything I could to get there. My focus was still all on basketball. Thinking back, it wasn't basketball God was trying to take away from me.

I remember being back in the states and the doctor there said it was perfectly healed. He put me on a 3-month physical therapy program to get me back in shape. I think God still wanted me to play but wanted also to wake me up and he gave me my leg back! I had no more pain, and was blessed with excellent healing.

I had the time and energy to put back into ball but it was a long road. I had to live life and face people even though I was done actually playing for a while. It wasn't sinking in. I didn't recognize the problem until a year later. I was just focused on getting back to level. God was trying to get my attention, though I didn't see it until the end of my sophomore season, which was a bad experience at a public school in the US. I was still putting my identity in basketball but it wasn't bringing anything. I wasn't getting what I wanted from it. It awakened me. It was a long process. My junior year was when I recognized my problem, accepted where I was and changed my mindset, realizing the past 2 years that basketball had affected my life negatively.

The coach we had that year had played in college and was really helping our team. Coach Derrick had an accident in college keeping him from playing too and he consistently said something that was very different from what the professional athletes said. They always said that basketball is more than a game, it's a passion. Derrick would say the best way you can look at it is, it's simply a game. I was skeptical...since I was under the influence of the passion.

Even though he said it was just a game he would push us a lot harder and hold us to high standards at practices. Saying it was just a game didn't mean he didn't want us to push for excellence but rather do so with the right mindset; not putting our whole identity into the game but letting excellence in the game come from something deeper.

After hearing his story of breaking an ankle then as he was recovering, breaking the other one, I saw a better philosophy. He could laugh at himself now but had paid for that lesson. He had twice the pain, twice the recovery, maybe twice the lessons that I had.

When I began to understand what he meant by the game really being just a game, I began to fathom his passion. It was a higher one, that encompassed all of life.

Sports have power to ruin people and change them into

self-exalting ones who react and treat people negatively, jeopardizing everything just for a game. I remember thinking that I had to have things in order in my life. I had to put God at the top of the list. But I like looking at it a bit differently; not having God at the top but at the center with everything else around him. You can do everything with God in the center where all the areas of our lives flow from him. Performance in basketball no longer had an effect on me off the court; it slowly sank in. I taught myself how to not let it affect all my life. I actually started performing better. It doesn't have to take away from the intensity and hard work. In fact, I put more work and intensity into it. When you're doing it for yourself, it's nowhere. When you have the right motives, there's so much more to it.

The next year I was able to coach U 11 and 13 teams. I began to use basketball as a common ground to be in kids' lives and speak in. I could see in younger kids how easily they would take a sport too seriously since I had been there. Now, I put far more time and work in than ever, but if I were depending on my performance for my identity, I wouldn't be playing. In an interview, Kobe Bryant said what drives him is being best. For me, I love pushing myself and working hard but it isn't the winning or the recognition that drives me. I just love to play and improve my skills and I still have my leg!" Kelvin Scott

We are all tempted to let other things define us and we work hard to hold up a certain banner over our lives proclaiming who we want people to think we are. When that doesn't pan out we're shaken and it's time to look at who God says we are.

~for growth~

From what are you most tempted to draw your identity?

What comes to mind to fill in the blank: if only I had __ I would be happy?

CHAPTER 26

WATCHING SELF

"Watch yourselves..."

GALATIANS 6:1, NIV

Dan was getting a check-up at the eye doctor and was encouraged to try the new progressive lenses even though he just wanted something for working at the computer. Lauding the claims of these state-of-the-art lenses, the woman convinced us he would be very happy to have a lens that was useful for varying ranges of sight if he would just try for two weeks. Well, the headaches and dizziness and general annoyance didn't let up, so we headed back in, told the technician he was having trouble and didn't think he wanted to continue with these lenses. She turned her head and reared back as if shouting a hamburger order and said to someone in the back, "We have a PROGRESSIVE NON-ADAPT!" I about died laughing but had to hold it in. She was serious. This customer of hers was not adapting to the progressive lenses and she seemed rather disappointed. We left with the ones he wanted in the first place. So now, when Dan doesn't like my ideas I just call him a progressive non-adapt.☺

It's just too good. I have to take it to another level.

How are we adapting to the progression God is seeking to make in our lives? Do we quickly give up at annoyances or conflicts that come along? Are we progressive non-adapts ☺ not willing to see through a lens that might give a clearer picture of ourselves?

Going back to the subject of greatness, if we do want to be great (a normal desire), we must take great care. We so easily get that wrong because we slap on our idea of greatness. Bigger, fancier, more...we think. That's not necessarily God's style of greatness. He often works greatness into people in an obscure way. His greatest moment hardly would've made the newspaper in the next town and was downplayed by the authorities until they had to make it look like a scam to save face. We need to check our definition of greatness often. We are pulled by the undertow of our need for self-justification, preservation, exaltation, or comfort. We often want to be great in the wrong ways.

Thus, the need for opening up ourselves for counsel, listening to others and watching ourselves and our teaching; for clueing in to the progress he wants to bring about in us. This is where we let others speak into our lives and take time and care to speak into theirs. It takes work and we need strength for it. We are fragile beings.

Maybe we avoid it because subconsciously we don't want to be scrutinized. We know how short we fall, so we're afraid to stick our necks out to help another, lest we end up having to take a look at our own blind spots too. Or it could just be an underlying laziness that keeps us hiding from needed change.

Change is rarely fun until you see the results. It could be

months later... but what a joy to sense that you are actually part-nering with God to change beliefs, and patterns of thought and behavior! By taking hold of his truth in our minds we "become partakers of the divine nature", recorded in 2 Peter 1:4. It is worth noting that in this same chapter Peter speaks about "making much effort" toward change. Our effort and our faith go together.

How much do we really work on these things? Are we satisfied to just miss out on so much expansion in our hearts? Where are the ones who put in fresh effort toward godliness (1 Timothy 4:7)? Who want it more than other things, like varsity athletes? They're the ones who are always at practice, who give up things to focus, who listen hard because they know they need to hear what the coach says if they're going to improve.

As a gymnast in my youth I remember hearing my coach's voice in my head as I was going through a routine and that enabled me to concentrate and do what I was supposed to do. It took a long time for each move to become habit and a very short time to revert to sloppiness.

Behind the combination of beautiful flow and amazing strength in a gymnast's moves are hours of focused discipline and sacrifice. Our coaches helped us "watch ourselves" to see where we were slacking when we didn't know it, where we needed extra effort and time. Can we gently, humbly, caringly do that for each other in our Christian lives? If done with care, it is a major cata-lyst to growth.

Feedback like this has to be sought. It has to be asked for. You've got to want it! And most often I don't. I'd rather not go there and mess up my fine ideas of myself. But would we hesitate if we knew there was disease in our bodies? Wouldn't we want an analysis and help with what to do about it? My husband and I knew we needed to delve into some intense evaluation as leaders feeling stuck and stale, so we enrolled in a week program that took us through our first 360 evaluation, some rigorous tests, interviews and self-examination. It was like soul surgery without the anesthesia!

As we were wading through this time I reached a point of haziness and confusion and happened to be in Psalm 51 that day. And in my scattered questioning thoughts, God interrupted, lifted my chin in his strong and gentle way. "You desire truth in the inmost being and in the hidden part You will make me know wisdom"! Psalm 51:6, NASB, Wow. A word straight and deep to my heart. He wants truth there where there are lies lurking dormant yet seeping. He will make me know wisdom there as I seek him and make effort to become a partaker of his nature. "Grace is not opposed to effort, it is opposed to earning." Dallas Willard

Another aspect of watching ourselves has to do with coming to grips with our own needs, our limits and accepting God's boundaries for us. There is freedom in limits. Submitting to these things in our lives is a gift. Taking time to receive from him is essential in order to have healthy souls.

This is often neglected in the name of selflessness but rarely without repercussions of burnout, strain, stress and disorientation. Remember how mad God was that the land didn't get the rest (Sabbath) it needed, let alone the people? That's one of the reasons he had to send his people into exile, to get their attention so they'd do things the way he meant for them to be done. It also happens to be what's best for our bodies and souls. We get much too practical and logical and assume our flurried ways are getting much more done than if we stopped to nurture our souls. I love Eugene Peterson's take on Sabbath in his excellent book Working the Angles, p. 72, 80. He talks about the rhythm of praying and playing. Nurturing connection with God - free of our routines -and enjoying Him, creation, and space to step away and "play". This reminds us that our work can be trusted into His hands. It's not about us and all we can do, because there are always obstacles and always more work.

How Joseph Learned to Watch Himself

Now the Joseph of Genesis, Jacob's eleventh son is a fascinating story of a young man literally thrown into a desperate and seemingly hopeless situation. He was about seventeen years of age and the day he wore his multi colored 'graduation' robe was a lot different than the day our kids wore theirs.

His family was in quite a dysfunctional state. Joseph had managed to bring out intense hatred from his brothers and they were about to be done with him. See, he had had some dreams about greatness and was a bit too verbal about them and it was only because of his older brother Reuben that he didn't die that day. He was instead thrown into a cistern and then taken and sold as a slave in Egypt.

No graduation party, no cross-cultural orientation, no member care or diploma, no phone. He was left and forgotten and thrown into an entirely different world and language, a genuine third culture kid (meaning he wasn't in the Hebrew culture anymore nor was he Egyptian so he was somewhere in between). His Dad wept for days when the brothers said a wild animal got him. Family life got worse.

Joseph was up against some major odds. Imagine the temptation to bitterness, hatred and ignoring God. We don't know how much he struggled and cried and begged God to get him out, but somehow, he came to grips with the fact that God let this happen. He chose to believe God was in it and was with him. And the amazing thing about the rest of the story is Joseph's response to his situation. After he is bought as a slave, something about him is noticed and he succeeds enough to be put in charge of his master's house. Then, in spite of keeping his integrity and resisting temptation, he is stripped of his position again, thrown in prison for a long time. Instead of (or after) pouting, he gets up and sweeps the floors and is again noticed and put in charge.

Since it really was somehow, ordained by God, the story of Joseph has profound things to say to us about God's sovereignty in our lives. As we all walk and struggle with knowing our God, consider Joseph's response to the abuse, humiliation and harm done to him in his life.

If we could learn one thing from Joseph let's learn that God allows stuff into our lives because it is his specific training plan for us, while fitting into his purposes. He is our "personal trainer, not our cosmetic surgeon"! (Russ Minick) Do you know the difference? If we can cooperate with God in every aspect of our lives, we'll move a lot farther, a lot faster toward what we were made to be.

Joseph had to learn to watch himself and his responses to God in the mess of his life, and even in prison people took notice! He handled temptation, loss, loneliness and success by connecting with God and fearing Him more than anything. Check out Genesis 41:46 to see when he got out of prison! His early dreams of greatness came about in a very different way than he would ever have wanted or imagined.

~for growth~

What keeps you from watching over your soul?

CHAPTER 27

EXCAVATING THE SOUL

"I have no special talents, I am only passionately curious."

Albert Einstein

In one of the journey groups I was leading, the young women began to call our meetings, "The Dig," as in an excavation. I thought it was an excellent depiction of what was happening in our souls. (DIG -Discipleship in Group)

It's amazing what the C#m (c sharp minor) musical chord can do to your soul. It gives an aura of mystery and depth, of longing for more of what's Real and beyond us. When you decide to join God in what he's doing in and around you, it's like a C# minor moment. ☺

In those moments it is good to take a deep look at where you've come from, what were the major influencing factors for good and bad and what conclusions you came to that may have led you off in the wrong direction or set the course for bad patterns of relating or given you subconscious resolve to think a certain way.

It is often the questions and accusations in the wee hours of the night that urge me to bring my groanings to God. At one juncture in my life, I journaled and wrestled with God, trying to put words to my introversion. Books and friends, little by little, mentored me through. I began charting a plan to help others walk through a journey of their lives so as to grasp more fully the story God wants to tell by their life. This eventually became a ten-session small group plan where we seek God together and help each other probe our lives and false beliefs. Every time I go through this with a group, I discover peoples' amazing stories. I discover more about God and myself.

This life debriefing is so lifting and can be redeeming. I'm finishing Dr. Wess Stafford's (a former president of Compassion International) book, Too Small to Ignore and my heart is still wrenching over what he had to go through as a young child and how this affected him and his parents. Wess was the victim of a poorly run and poorly supervised mission school. I ask God, "why didn't you answer the cries of this little boy?" But we forget.

Because of what Wess suffered and what he experienced living among the poor, there are tens of thousands of kids being helped today. Because he chose to learn from and share those sufferings. We forget the depths of what is learned in suffering and tend to want to just eliminate it. This goes so against our grain. There is gift in suffering that God wants to use for our diseased and pain-ridden world. We are rebels against this fallen world. And it takes a fight. I'm so grateful for people like Wess, and many others who take the trauma of their early lives and let God make a trophy of grace. God does the impossible. Notice that most of the leaders in the Bible went through immense suffering. We tend to want to gloss over our pasts because of sin and shame, but that's what God wants to redeem to show the world that he is greater. He did answer Wess' prayers as a little boy. Just not how we would have planned it. Some questions we have to leave with Him.

In our well-intentioned zeal or our rigorous sense of duty we can so often miss the voice of God into our souls. Our enemy accuses of self-serving when we obey the Scriptures regarding "watching over our hearts with all diligence," Proverbs 4:23, NASB. Yet at the expense of appearing selfishly introspective we must obey and draw near to God as we seek truth "in our innermost parts," Psalm 51:6, ISV. This quote stirs me to this.

"Become acquainted with your own heart. Though it is deep probe it. Though it is obscure, search it. Though it deceives us, giving other names to its sicknesses, do not trust it. If people did not remain strangers to themselves, they would not maintain all their lives in the same paralyzed state. But they give faltering names to their own natural weaknesses. They try to justify, palliate, or excuse the evils of their own hearts, rather than uproot and destroy them ruthlessly. They never gain a realistic view of themselves. Ineffective lives and scandal grow like branches out of this root of self-ignorance. How few truly seek to know themselves or possess the courage to do so."
Sin and Temptation, John Owen pp.131,132.

We have to want to work on ourselves, and God calls us to it. Conforming us to His image often takes our participation. "Salvation is not merely a gift received once for all; it expresses itself in an ongoing process in which the believer is strenuously involved." (NIV Study Bible note on Philippians 2:12)

We are all broken because of the evil of our world. But we become more of what he made us to be as he "transforms us from glory to glory." 2 Corinthians 3:18, author's paraphrase. After one of our "Dig" sessions I wrote to the group,

"I've already gotten my ears opened to some rebukes, one being a sense of spiritual entitlement. This is really embarrassing before God because I know in my head that anything I have, I have received! Yet somehow, I found myself feeling entitled to greater power or help because I have been following him so long and served him in hard places. It is absurd that I even entertain such things but He is gracious to show me."

Are you hearing anything new from him as you listen to him in the inner sanctuary of your heart where he dwells? Are you noticing anything he's trying to point out as you look at your journey? We do need to ask for alertness to his still small voice as we're in the Word, with others; as we observe ourselves and our reactions. In his creation around us, and as thoughts come into your minds, ask for his Spirit to lead you into the truth you need in order to be freed.

~for growth~

From Dallas Willard on guidance and hearing from God:

- We are important enough to God for him to speak to us.
- His speaking to us does not in itself make us important.
- When God speaks to us, it does not prove that we are righteous or even right. It does not even prove that we have correctly understood what he said. The infallibility of the messenger and the message does not guarantee the infallibility of our reception. Humility is always in order. This is an especially important point to make since the appeals "God told me" or "the Lord led me" are commonly used by the speaker to prove that "I am right" or "you should follow me" or "I should get my way."

"Some of Jesus' deepest teachings are about hearing...he urged his hearers to make a great effort to hear, assuring them that what they received would be proportional to their desire and effort."

(MARK 4:23, 24) HEARING GOD, PP. 37-39

YOUR LIFE IS RE-MARKABLE

I have seen that taking the time to gather and explore life with other trusted seekers has provided great leaps in growth, freedom and joy. May these glimpses from my life be an impetus for you to do some soul exploring!

One way to go about that is through journey coaching.

Journey Coaching

A small group journey together to unearth deep-seated beliefs that affect our lives and to give insight toward walking in love and freedom.

These sessions are done by invitation for those committed to going deeper in exploring their lives and spirituality over a period of ten ninety-minute sessions.

PURPOSE:

identify a growth area in my life where God wants to work;

recognize the lies that I have lived by regarding that area

work with God to uproot those lies and plant His truth.

"Behold, You desire truth in the innermost being, and in the hidden part You will make me know wisdom."
PSALM 51:6, NASB

These sessions include:

Taking a look (*Psalm 139:23, 24*)
It's Biblical to "work" on ourselves
We need to choose to work with God on ourselves
The enemy is prowling yet God's power over him
is our hope.

Probing our lives (*Lamentations 3:40*)
Beginning to hear our self-talk

Digging deeper into our patterns and beliefs (*1 Timothy 4:16*)
Life journey lines/early foundations

Innermost Being (*Ephesians 4: 22-24*)
Fighting the lies/renewing our minds

Battle Within (*2 Corinthians 10:4,5*)
Walking in the Spirit/recognizing the schemes of
the enemy

Overcoming (*Romans 8:37*)
Accepting trials as tools and becoming conquerors
through his love

View of God & Self (*2 Corinthians 3:18*)
Examining our views of God and self as we deeply
experience the truth of God's Spirit and living
Word

Transforming (*Romans 12:1,2*)
Setting our minds on the Spirit/going to the hard
places

"Plunder" & Purpose (*John 10:10*)
Keeping our freedom from slavery to our old ways

Celebration & Resilience (*Exodus 15*)
Remembering and Planning

Gordon McDonald in his book, <u>A Resilient Life</u> p. 98 says,

"We carry within ourselves all our yesterdays, the experiences and influences that have happened from our birth to this present moment. These yesterdays can powerfully affect today, the right-now and dominate our relationships, our choices, our view of ourselves, and even our understanding of God. If our yesterdays are in a state of good repair, they provide strength for today. If not repaired, they create havoc."

Responses from past groups:

This journey group gave me the motivation and support to unearth deep lies and to begin to allow God in to redeem and restore. That is what I want more than anything; to walk in a way that is beautiful to the Lord. I know that I will get nowhere by continuing in the lies that I have identified. I wrote some of the claims that I am working on believing in my heart. I feel that my heart is often stubborn and slow to accept truth and often more comfortable hanging onto negativity or arguments to support old lies. But it is a journey and I feel that these messages of truth are slowly penetrating.

It has guided and encouraged me in heart changes that I would not have done alone or without the wisdom from others who have experience walking with the Lord. I didn't know what I was missing! Having your eyes opened to blind areas in your life is hard but having a spiritually mature coach gives you permission to look into those areas with confidence God won't abandon you during the process. The prayers have opened my heart to communing with God in ways I have not known before and it's been something I have shared with others each week. Practicing and doing them together has been a huge encouragement despite how vulnerable it makes me feel. Hearing others talk with God and how they relate with Him gives the group a connection I don't think would be there otherwise.

It gave me a renewed ability to focus and straighten my priorities on what needed to be worked on. It opened my eyes to my own life and past and hurts that impact me on a daily basis and gave me the ability and opportunity to reflect on my life and who I am. It has opened my eyes to things from my past that need to change to bring me closer to the woman that God has made me to be.

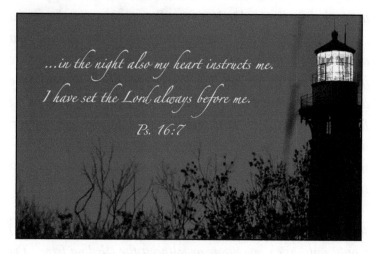

Photo - Eric Froelich

For more info on journey groups or leading a journey group visit www.soulfit.us. If you are interested in a 30-minute free exploratory session, indicate with the contact form on the website. Individual and group coaching available. Facilitator guide available.

May your life journey be deeper, richer and more joyful than you ever imagined it could be! I would love to hear from you.

Jackie
www.soulfit.us

Jacqueline Scott MA
Life Coach ACC

ICF

ACKNOWLEDGEMENTS

"There is no success without sacrifice. If you succeed without sacrifice it is because someone has suffered before you. If you sacrifice without success it is because someone will succeed after."

Adoniram Judson

With the arrival of our first grandchild in the year of 2019, I'm being drawn to the past and to the future. I'm zooming out to take a look at this phenomenon called life. My little part, my story, is a drop in a huge generational wave of people who have gone before, of whose lives I am somehow a beneficiary. What do we need to learn from the vast humanity that went before us? Who do we need to "meet" from our pasts? Will those who come after us, learn from us? Will they realize how we struggled to find our way and prayed for them to find the Way?

I'm intrigued with my grandparents, yet know so little about them. It was a different and distant world they occupied. I'm especially drawn to my paternal grandmother, Baba, we called her, in the few fleeting memories I have of her. So young when she took on a new world, a new identity, a daunting adventure along with the certain hardship and suffering of an immigrant.

Having lived most of my adult life on the side of the world she came from, I gasp in relief that she left when she did, seeing now the aftermath of the soul-draining and humanity-stripping life brought about by communism. I live among them in the leftovers and rubble of an ideology gone bad.

This is a small tribute to Mary Hutsko who came to the USA from the Ukraine in 1911 at the age of sixteen.

"In the last quarter of the nineteenth century, mass emigration was also taking place from western Ukraine to the Americas. Rural overpopulation, poverty, malnutrition, a high mortality rate, and unemployment were among the factors that precipitated outmigration at that time. Also at work were pull factors, including stories of great economic opportunities in the West - often exaggerated by the shipping agents who recruited immigrants, primarily for work in Pennsylvania's coal mines."

"The emigrants, predominantly poor peasants and young single people, hoped to earn enough money to pay for the voyage and all their existing debts, and to save enough to return to Ukraine, buy land, and establish themselves as farmers. Later, most emigrants expected to settle permanently in the United States...

"...immigration policies of the host countries at that time were liberal ...labor was in great demand for industry in the United States."

"...in their own homeland they fought hard to preserve their native language, religious beliefs, customs and traditions that were constantly being threatened by foreign domination."

Ukrainian immigration: A Study in EthnicSurvival* Ann Lencyk Pawliczko

United Nations Population Division https://onlinelibrary.wiley.com/doi/pdf/10.1111/j.2050-411X.1994.tb00104.x

I imagine her having the fascination of a young girl, along with the terror of heading across an unknown ocean, arriving at the port, stepping tremblingly aboard the crowded steerage of a ship with who-knows-what kind of provisions. Fleeing demise, dreaming of dignity, perhaps she was full of hope and fearful courage, at the same time carrying the disillusionment of life as it was. She had no idea of the sacrifice and battering that life would bring.

"Before World War I, 98 percent of Ukrainians settled in the northeastern states, with 70 percent in Pennsylvania."

Read more: https://www.everyculture.com/multi/Sr-Z/Ukrainian-Americans.html#ixzz5lvXegwkM

As exhilarating as it might have been to finally reach America, the inspection station at Ellis Island surely had its cold stares and strange languages to face. Some were sent back upon arrival. I wonder how long she had to wait, what kind of welcome she had, what prejudices and anxieties she had to push through.

I'm told she worked as a nanny for a while, then married. Life was grueling, and work for my grandfather in the coal mine was abusive. My father, the tenth child, doesn't remember a conversation with his father who died young of black lung disease. He worked twelve hours a day in the mines of Eastern Pennsylvania and smoked a pipe after work at night. Their lives were completely poured out for the next generation.

Although my grandparents were distant and a mystery to me, I want to thank them. I want to tell them it was worth it. Surely, they had hopes and dreams and capabilities. They certainly accomplished much, unobtrusively inaugurating life in a new land, surviving the Great Depression. But the seeds of their personal aspirations were regretfully buried in the soil of the future, watered with unseen tears. Look at what they started! Look at what has come because they braved the voyage into the luring and looming unknown! A diverse wave of Ukrainian and half-Ukrainian descendants. Those seeds cracking, bursting, sprouting and fruitful in their children, grandchildren and great grandchildren. But they didn't get to see it.

Atrocities of hidden history still leak out of fragmented lives here in the post-Soviet milieu; crippling thought patterns amid floundering newfound freedoms. The past stays with us for a long time. It's in our bones and our DNA, but it will soon be a distant memory. What will my grandchildren know of me in 100 years?!

When I asked some relatives what her life might have been like, my cousin replied "What do you think it was like? She had 10 kids!?" ☺ I'm told she loved to cook and garden and I understand church was a big part of their community life.

How much we have gained from these unknowing valiant ones! They paved a way for us to live our lives as they wished they could have lived theirs. Let's not forget that.

Jackie (Hutsko) Scott

> "Children are the living messages we send to a time we will not see."
>
> Neil Postman

The stories in this book are a smattering of awakened moments. Part of the joy of writing is bringing back memories of valiant, ordinary people with deep wells of pain and beauty, who extraordinarily affected me. There are too many to name. Here are some I must mention:

To my parents, Dr. Joseph & JoAnne Hutsko – How can we

ever know the far-reaching grasp that our DNA and our early forming have on us? In both of you there was a fight to overcome, to step into the potential you'd been given. Somehow that was infused in me. Thank you.

To Calvary Church in Coopersburg, PA, you creatively reached out to the kids in your community and God captured my heart.

Thank you to Ellen Peters for your keen editing eye and for being the first to help me dig out of the trenches of self.

And to Eric Peters, our stellar leader for so many years, who said to me, "God uses you to take us into his word." Do you know how much that encouraged and empowered me?

To my sisters, Patty, Chrissy and Lynn, such huge hearts and overcoming spirits, ever my cheerleaders, even though I bossed you around so much in our youth.

To my incredible sons Luke, Brad & Kelv, each so unique and creative, each spurring me on, and acting like I'm some kind of wonder woman.

To Rachie, my remarkable daughter who had the foresight to see the need to delve into doing journey groups virtually and whose early quest for truth, sent me deeper into mine.

To Dan, my confidante, whose courage and charge into life lifts me, awakens me and challenges me to be who I'm made to be. Thank you for the hours you didn't have, yet you put into editing and suggestions, acting like I had something to say!

To my God, for your close, kind promptings and pulls; for your assuring embrace, your deep energetic love and your calling for me to go with you into others' hearts as well as into my own.

ABOUT THE AUTHOR

Photo courtesy of Cheri Magarrel

Jacqueline Scott grew up in Pennsylvania, USA, was capti-
vated by God at age 12; became an RN, got a BS in Bible, then
a Masters in Leadership Studies. While in university she met Dan
then headed to Bolivia, South America to save the world. She
had four kids instead. ☺ They moved to Central Asia in 1994 in
leadership with a non-profit agency. Currently credentialed as a
personal and leader development coach, she works with individ-
uals and groups in person and on-line.

CPSIA information can be obtained
at www.ICGtesting.com
Printed in the USA
LVHW080545100920
665470LV00002B/4